BALLYMALOE

The History of a Place and its People

September 2022

BALLYMALOE

The History of a Place and its People

JANE HAYTER-HAMES

Thank you for joining my tour to-day!

Fern Allen

Rushford Publishing

First published by Rushford Publishing, Chagford, 2016
Reprinted 2018
sales@rushfordpublishing.co.uk

ISBN: 978-1-5262-0106-5

Printed by Gutenberg Press, Tarxien, Malta

Contents

List of Illustrations   vii

List of Maps   xi

List of Plans   xiii

Acknowledgements   xv

1.   Prehistory   1
2.   The Saint Arrives   8
3.   Invaders   16
4.   Norman Settlers at Ballymaloe   21
5.   The Seneschal and the Dean   27
6.   Sir John FitzEdmund FitzGerald   36
7.   Lady Honora and Young Sir John   56
8.   The War of Three Kingdoms   66
9.   A Boyle House   75
10. Colonel Edward Corker   85
11. Gentlemen of Business   93
12. Mr Litchfield, Gentleman Farmer   106
13. Captain Simpson and His Family   118
14. The Allens of Ballymaloe   128

Appendices: Poems of St Colmán   141
                The FitzGerald of Cloyne Harp – Inscriptions   142
                Verses on the Portrait of Chuffe   143
                Changes to the Buildings at Ballymaloe Made by the Allens   144
                The Walled Garden   146
                Ballymaloe Owners and Occupiers   149

Select Bibliography   150

Index   154

List of Illustrations

1. Giant Irish deer, artist's impression. © Iona Tweedie. — 2

2. Antlers of giant Irish deer in the hall at Ballymaloe House. — 3

3. Stone Age axe-heads at Ballymaloe House. — 4

4. Cloyne discs from Carrigacrump, near Cloyne. © The National Museum of Ireland. — 5

5. Gold lunula, undecorated, 2200–2000 B.C., Middleton, Co. Cork. © Ashmolean Museum, University of Oxford. — 5

6. West end of Ballymaloe House showing the turret. — 31

Between pages 76–77

7. Cloyne Cathedral.

8. Barryscourt Castle, a restored tower house.

9. The gargoyle on the turret.

10. The stairs within the turret.

11. Chamber within the turret.

12. The gate house from within the yard.

13. The gate house from without.

14. Charles Blount, 8th Baron Mountjoy, Lord Deputy of Ireland. © The Trustees of the British Museum.

15. Sir John FitzEdmund FitzGerald's carved stone at Ballymaloe House.

16. Sir John FitzEdmund's stone on the arch at Ballymaloe.

17. Sir John FitzEdmund's stone at Cloyne House.

18. Map of Imokilly, made for George Carew, Lord President of Munster, early 17th century. © The Board of Trinity College, Dublin.

19. The FitzGerald Harp, replica at Ballymaloe House.

20. The statue of the Virgin in the silver gilt shrine given by Lady Honora FitzGerald, St Mary's Church, Pope's Quay, Cork.

21. Earl of Castlehaven. Possibly James Touchet, 3rd Earl of Castlehaven attributed to Sir Peter Lely, oil on canvas, circa 1640s. Photograph, © National Portrait Gallery, London, unknown collection (NPG Z18101).

22. Murrough O'Brien, 1st Earl of Inchiquin, by John Michael Wright. By kind permission of Manchester Art Gallery.

23. Roger Boyle, 1st Earl of Orrery, after a portrait of 1660 (engraving), English School, 17th century. © Private Collection / Bridgeman Images.

24. Margaret, Countess of Orrery. By permission of Mary Evans Picture Library.

25. Portrait of Lady Mary Boyle (1566–1673) and her son Charles Boyle (d.1720) oil on canvas, studio of Sir Godfrey Kneller. Private Collection, © Lawrence Steigrad Fine Arts, New York / Bridgeman Images.

26. Colonel Henry Boyle. © By kind permission of Harry Boyle, 10th Earl of Shannon.

27. Sir Thomas Dilkes. © National Maritime Museum, Greenwich, London – Greenwich Hospital Collection.

28. The Queen Anne wing from the stable yard.

29. The Queen Anne wing from the front of the house.

30. The archway from within the yard and without.

31. Colonel Corker's carved stone in the apex of the arch.

32. The front entrance to the courtyard.

33. The cellar showing the rocky outcrop.

34. Portrait of Chuffe by J. Flynn at Ballymaloe.

35. The Jester, painting at Ballymaloe.

36. Map of Ballymaloe townland, from Griffiths Valuation 1845–1864. Ordnance Survey, Ireland.

37. Map of Ballymaloe from the sale particulars of 1883.

38. Portrait of a Litchfield son.

39. Portrait of a Litchfield duaghter.

40. Embroidered bodice belonging to the Litchfields.

41. Butter pats used by Helen Morgan (née Simpson) as a girl.

42. Charles Simpson with Dorothy on the bridge over the River Rooskah behind Ballymaloe.

43. Outside the main entrance looking down the road to Cloyne.

44. Larry Neill the coachman in the yard.

45. Ballymaloe House from the west.

46. Harvesting.

47. The pony trap coming up the drive.

48. Bill Neill in the farmyard.

Between pages 108–109

49. William Litchfield's farming diary. By kind permission of Rory Allen.

50. Wilson Strangman. © Newtown School, Waterford.

51. Ballymaloe House in the early twentieth century.

52. Muriel and Terence McSwiney with their daughter. Photograph, Cork Public Museum.

53. Captain Jim Simpson.

54. Jim Simpson and Helen at her wedding to Tom Morgan, Midleton, spring 1952.

55. Helen Simpson in the Litchfield veil.

56. Wedding Group, Helen Simpson's marriage to Tom Morgan, 1952.

57. Sale Particulars for Ballymaloe, 1947.

58. Ivan Allen with jersey herd.

59. Jersey herd on the avenue.

60. Ivan Allen with the milking machine.

61. The Allen family c. 1958.

62. Rory and Tim Allen on top of a car.

63. The driveway as it was in the 1950s.

64. The front façade in the 1950s with Ivan, Myrtle and friends.

65. The Allen family in 1977.

66. Myrtle Allen cooking.

67. Anne MacCarthy in the Yeats Room.

68. Joe Cronin delivering the post.

69. Joe and Rita Cronin in 1991.

70. The dessert trolley.

71. Ballymaloe House as night falls 2015. Photograph Joleen Cronin.

72. Explore Ballymaloe. Map © Marina Langer.

73. Hazel Allen.

74. Rory Allen on guitar in the hall.

75. President Bill Clinton on stage in the Grainstore at the Worldwide Ireland Funds Conference in 2012.

76. President Bill Clinton with Mrs Allen.

77. The drawing room.

78. The dining room.
79. The courtyard.
80. The green drawing room.
81. The roof.
82. From the roof, 2015.
83. The swimming pool.
84. The walled garden.
85. The kitchen.
86. The conservatory, long room and the new bedrooms.

Picture Credits

Illustrations Nos 2, 3, 9–12, 15, 19, 28, 30, 32–35, 77–86.
Photographs © Dara McGrath
Illustrations Nos 6–8, 13, 16, 17, 20, 29, 31. Photographs © Jane Hayter-Hames
Illustrations Nos 42–48, 51, 53–56. Photographs © Helen Morgan
Illustrations Nos 57–71, 73–76. Photographs © Ballymaloe House Archive
All other illustrations are by permission and copyright as shown.

All maps and plans by John Plumer of JP Map Graphics Ltd.

List of Maps

1. Munster   xviii–xix
2. The Prehistoric Record   6
3. Early Christian Munster   10
4. South-East Ireland in the Viking Era   17
5. Imokilly – 14th and 15th Centuries   23
6. Church and County Boundaries   29
7. The Early Modern Wars in Munster   54
8. East Cork – modern   124

List of Plans

1. The tower house, 15th – 16th century   33
2. Sir John FitzEdmund FitzGerald's house, late 16th – early 17th century   59
3. The house with the Queen Anne wing, c. 1709   88
4. The house after the Morrison extension was added in the early 18th century   97
5. The layout of Ballymaloe 1923–1947, by Priscilla Oldfield   120–121

Acknowledgements

I am very grateful to Rory and Hazel Allen for asking me to write a history of Ballymaloe, and for all the help they have given me. I took up a great deal of Rory's time trying to piece together the architectural history of the house. We were helped enormously by Frank Keohane whose expertise was invaluable and who gave generously of his time, and by the late Jeremy Williams with his exceptional memory for buildings and people. Professor Tadhg O'Keeffe brought a different perspective, for which many thanks.

Professor John A Murphy agreed to read the manuscript and I am very grateful for his patient and thoughtful advice. Maria O'Donovan of Cork University Press advised me from the beginning and throughout the process of making this book. Without her skill and expertise it would be a far inferior production.

I could hardly have tackled the twentieth-century history of Ballymaloe without the help of Helen Morgan, who grew up in the house and was unstinting in giving her memories and support. We had splendid conversations. I also visited her sister, Priscilla Oldfield, who was wonderfully helpful and provided documents and photographs, as well as her own plans of the house showing the layout of the rooms. Sadly she died while the book was in production. Helen's daughter Liz Cotter made time to help me with illustrations and I am very grateful to her for all her support.

Harry Boyle, 10th Earl of Shannon, generously provided a copy of his portrait of Colonel Henry Boyle for which I am grateful.

I had encouragement and support from all the Allen family at Ballymaloe, for which I would like to express my thanks. Wendy, Tash, Tim, Yasmin and Fern all read what I wrote about their family at Ballymaloe and helped me improve it, as did Rory and Hazel.

Joe Cronin gave me valuable information about Imokilly Orchards and farming at Ballymaloe. I am very grateful for all his help and encouragement.

Dr Michael Ryan, Pauline MacCarthy and Helen Cuddigan all helped me with illustrations – thank you. Dara McGrath went to a great deal of trouble with the photography and helped me with archival pictures, for which many thanks. Iona Tweedie did a drawing for me and Chris Chapman helped me with my own photography – thank you to both of them.

Richard Wood's memoirs were evocative and Stephen Pearce's full of information. Thank you to both of them for their time and anecdotes.

Dr Paul MacCotter, whose work on Cloyne was invaluable, also gave me permission to quote two of Colmán of Cloyne's poems, which Professor Donnchadh Ó Corráin translated for Paul's study of the saint, and I am very grateful to him.

My indefatigable copy-editor Aonghus Meaney straightened out many a slip and inconsistency, as well as all the references, for which many thanks. I would also like to thank John Plumer of JP Map Graphics who made the maps and plans, Alison Burns who designed the cover and Liz Hammond for proofreading.

The staff of all the libraries I have used have been very helpful. My thanks to Cork County Library, the National Library of Ireland with special thanks to Gerry Kavanagh, the Registry of Deeds and National Archives in Dublin, and the Bodleian Library in Oxford; also West Sussex Records Office and Dublin City Library. At Cork Archives, Brian McGee gave me tremendous assistance, as did Timmy O'Connor, with Peter and Michael. The staff of Boole Library at University College Cork were very helpful and supportive throughout the project, so warmest thanks to Elaine Harrington, Mary Lombard and Sheyeda Allen.

I would also like to thank Brenda Murphy and Barry Supple of Castlemartyr Resort, and Peter Murray and Fiona O'Brien at the Crawford Art Gallery.

I had planned to publish this book in print without footnotes, and online with them. For technical reasons, I have not done that. I hope the footnotes will not interrupt the reader's eye, but will be useful to local historians.

This book might have taken other forms, something which Rory, Hazel and I discussed when I began work. However, Rory's aim was that everything that could be known about Ballymaloe should be collected between two covers. I took that as my brief. The book naturally touches on wider Irish history and frequently ranges over local history, which seems necessary to make it intelligible. Although so many people have helped me, I am entirely responsible for the deductions made and the way that the story has been recorded.

BALLYMALOE

The History of a Place and its People

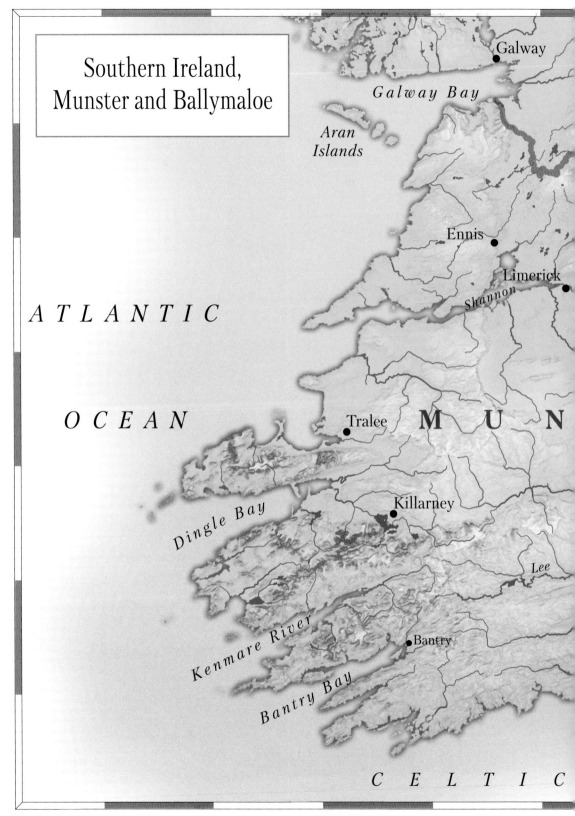

Southern Ireland,
Munster and Ballymaloe

Galway

Galway Bay

Aran
Islands

Ennis

Limerick

Shannon

ATLANTIC

OCEAN

Tralee

M U N

Killarney

Dingle Bay

Lee

Kenmare River

Bantry

Bantry Bay

CELTIC

Map 1.

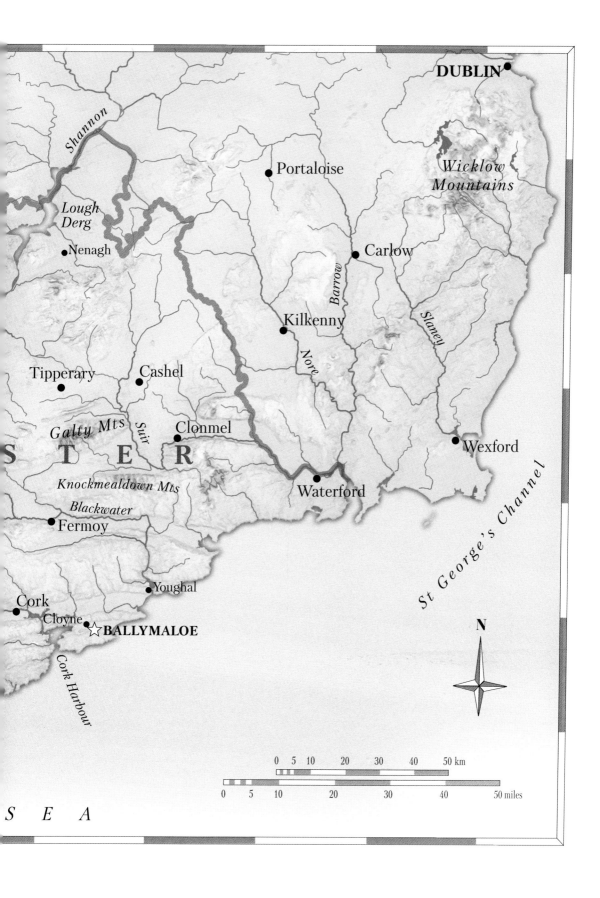

DUBLIN

Shannon

Portaloise

Wicklow Mountains

Lough Derg

Nenagh

Carlow

Barrow

Kilkenny

Slaney

Nore

Tipperary

Cashel

S   T   E   R

Galty Mts

Suir

Clonmel

Knockmealdown Mts

Wexford

Blackwater

Waterford

Fermoy

St George's Channel

Youghal

Cork

Cloyne

☆**BALLYMALOE**

N

Cork Harbour

0 5 10   20   30   40   50 km

0   5   10   20   30   40   50 miles

S   E   A

CHAPTER ONE

Prehistory

Ballymaloe – the name of the place has remained constant for many centuries, despite enormous changes in the local area and across Ireland. In Irish it is written Baile Uí Mhaolmhuaidh although the spelling can vary. Baile is a town, farmstead or settlement and Mhaolmhuaidh – pronounced Mo Lua – is the land-holder's name.[1]

Mo Lua left his name on his home and land in early medieval times. Over the centuries the original Irish word has been written in many ways – not only because Irish spellings varied, but because Church officials, tax collectors and administrators, writing in Latin or English, struggled with the complex sounds of the Irish language.

He had good land, the man who left his name here or the many generations of his family who created a fine farm in this place. They were starting from good bedrock, the free-draining limestone of the Cloyne valley beside the Rooskagh River. A spring of clear water bubbled up beside the river, giving the settlement an easy and reliable water supply. But the people who farmed at Ballymaloe were using land over which animal herds and earlier people had moved for many centuries.

It is worth going back to dwell on those early peoples and the animals which they hunted because both animals and humans have left spectacular remains. Ireland is at the very edge of Europe and the mammals moved in here as part of their great migrations from the south and east. Humans probably came into Ireland following the herds of animals which they hunted.

In the hall at Ballymaloe are the antlers of a giant deer which were found in Ballindotha bog to the south-east of the house at the bottom of the farm. The Megaloceros giganteus stood about two metres high at the shoulder and needed

---

[1] www.logainm.ie; Dr É. Lankford, *A Collection of Placenames from Cork County*, vol. 3 (Cork, 2008). Parish of Kilmahon.

1.　Giant Irish deer, artist's impression. Iona Tweedie.

abundant food supplies. They were in Ireland before the last glaciation – possibly 32,000 years ago – before Ireland and Britain had been separated by sea.[2] The giant deer lived in a belt of grassland between the sparse tundra of the north and the forest belt to the south. Here there was rich fodder with shrubs and berries among the grasses, on all of which they thrived. But the warm conditions did not last and as the climate deteriorated the giant deer moved south. They had to stay in the grasslands as tundra was too meagre for them and in the forest they could not manoeuvre because of their antlers. As the cold came south, they went further south – as it retreated, the giant deer returned to Ireland. However, by about 10,000 years ago the rich grasslands on which they depended were disappearing in Ireland and the giant deer began to die out in Western Europe.[3]

The great antlers of these creatures are made of bone and are often found in bogs because they were sealed there under the deepest level of clay which preserved them. They may have foundered in the marshy fringes of the pools as they came down to drink, their great heads pulling them forward. Or it may just be the special conditions of bog over clay which preserved the remains of animals which once were common in the grasslands of southern Ireland, but now found food scarce and had predators and competitors.

They were gone before the first humans came into Ireland. As the ice retreated the humans moved north and west across Europe but the grasslands had gone. Those old hunters may have come into what is now east Cork before there was sea

---

[2]　P.C. Woodman and N. Monaghan, 'From Mice to Mammoths: Dating Ireland's Earliest Faunas', *Archaeology Ireland*, vol. 7, no. 3, 1993, pp. 31–3.

[3]　F. Mitchell and M. Ryan, *Reading the Irish Landscape* (Dublin, 1997), pp. 87–93.

2. *Antlers of giant Irish deer in the hall at Ballymaloe House.*

between Britain and Ireland, but as the ice melted the land shifted and gradually the sea flowed into deep rifts in the land to create the Irish Sea.

The shoreline of east Cork emerged and just inland was the fertile Cloyne valley in which Ballymaloe now stands. Trees had colonised the island, with deer and wild pig, wolves and hare. The humans who followed them lived by hunting and gathering. Around Cork harbour piles of shells have been found where the early people scavenged for shellfish.[4] They left their axe-heads on the Ballymaloe land; some were found dating from the New Stone Age and are on display in the house. The polished stone heads were mounted into wooden hafts for use as an axe or a hoe because men had begun to cut down trees. Other stone tools were used for skinning game or cutting meat.

People started to farm in the fourth century BC and the land at Ballymaloe was ideal. Clearing the land was a massive task, cutting trees and extracting their roots, breaking up the soil. But new knowledge was spreading across Europe from the east: the valuable skills of metal-working. When those skills arrived in Ireland around 2,000 BC an extraordinary culture developed. The use of copper and its alloy bronze gave the early people wonderful new tools, but they also delighted in making beautiful metal artefacts with which to adorn themselves. In the Irish Bronze Age, a style of gold work developed which still dazzles us today.

---

[4] D. Power, comp. *Archaeological Inventory of County Cork, Volume 2: East and South Cork*, (Dublin, 1992), p. 69.

3. *Stone Age axe-heads.*

We know that these skills were being practised around east Cork because samples were found in the nineteenth century close to Ballymaloe. Bronze Age people lived on the fertile land of east Cork and had probably opened clearings in the forest so that they could farm the Cloyne valley. One of those clearings would later become the farmstead of Ballymaloe.

Those Bronze Age people left behind them a few samples of their golden jewellery and a more extraordinary artefact, a shroud made of tiny panels of beaten gold. The antiquarian Crofton Croker never saw it whole but he gave an account of what happened at Knockane near Castlemartyr, only a few miles from Ballymaloe:

> A curious discovery was made not far from Castlemartyr by a quarryman; in consequence of the crowbar having accidentally fallen through a fissure in the rock, he widened the aperture and descended in search of the instrument into a cavern, where he was not a little surprised to behold a human skeleton, partly covered with exceedingly thin plates of stamped or embossed gold, connected by bits of wire. He also found several amber beads.[5]

5   T.C. Croker, *Researches in the South of Ireland* (London, 1824), p. 253.

4.   *Cloyne discs from Carrigacrump, near Cloyne.*
This image is reproduced with the kind permission of the National Museum of Ireland.

Very little of this golden shroud survived. It was melted down and sold by the man who found it; only one tiny gold plate and a fragment of an amber bead were rescued and sold to the National Museum in Dublin. A similar find from Muskerry to the west was also crumpled up and brought for sale in Cork.

John Windele, the well-known antiquarian, said it 'would make the tender and sensitive heart of any antiquary bleed and bring down tears from his eyes'.[6] It was a great loss.

5.   *Gold lunula, undecorated, 2200–2000 BC, Midleton, Co. Cork.*

© Ashmolean Museum, University of Oxford.

---

6   M. Cahill, 'John Windele's Golden Legacy: Prehistoric and Later Gold Ornaments from Co. Cork and Co. Waterford', *Proceedings of the Royal Irish Academy*, section C, vol. 106C (Dublin, 2006), p. 255.

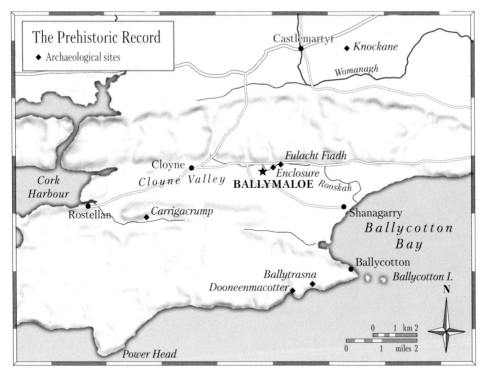

Map 2.

The golden shrouds were grave goods for the great men who lived here in those times, but the living also had magnificent pieces of gold jewellery. Near Cloyne a pair of gold discs were found in a cave at Carrigacrump. The discs, like the plaque for the skeleton, were decorated and each had a hole in the middle. They seem to have been sewn onto clothes. All these artefacts were made from fine sheets of gold and had been decorated by beating a delicate pattern into the metal.

The most spectacular Bronze Age finds from east Cork were the three gold necklaces or lunulae found near Midleton. One was given to the Ashmolean Museum in Oxford where it is part of their permanent display.

The gold probably came from the Wicklow mountains but wherever it came from, it had been carefully worked into gorgeous decorative objects. Someone held sway in the area around Ballymaloe whose goldsmiths had rare skills and the time to pursue them. This suggests that farmers were producing a surplus and that the ruler could support highly skilled craftsmen. Whatever else he had in fabrics, vessels or furniture we shall never see but perhaps can imagine.

Remnants of ancient hearths or fulacht fiadh were found in the fields to the east of Ballymaloe, said to date from the Bronze Age, so we can be fairly sure there was a settlement here in that period, perhaps temporary or for part of the year, perhaps as part of clearance and permanent settlement.

Long after other parts of Europe had turned to iron as a stronger metal, the Irish continued to perfect their bronze and gold artefacts.

Then, when iron swords began to appear in Ireland, it was in Ulster, not in the south. The Iron Age began around 300 BC in Ulster and the north. Iron Age peoples spoke Gaelic and had better weapons and tools, yet in Munster there is no trace of their culture for several centuries. It was around the time of Christ that the whole island started to exhibit a similar culture.[7] By then, Gaelic was spoken all over the island and iron was in use for farming, which was improving rapidly. More people may have arrived by sea; the nearby ruins of coastal forts at Ballytrasna and Dooneenmacotter may date from this time, suggesting some insecurity.

Ulster produced heroic tales such as *Táin Bó Cúailnge*, the story of an epic cattle raid, which give a vivid picture of ancient Gaelic Ireland. Many of Louis le Brocquy's prints which illustrate the story hang in Ballymaloe House.[8] We have few stories from Munster from that time to bring alive the local scene; not until the genealogies of the kings begin do we hear tales of rivalries and triumphs between the small kingdoms of our area.

Then we start to know the names of the people who lived in east Cork and we hear of an unusual man who was sent by the king to live on this peninsula. His settlement would set the pattern for life at Ballymaloe for a long time to come.

---

[7] B. Cunliffe, *Facing the Ocean: The Atlantic and its Peoples* (Oxford, 2001), pp. 359–64; B. Raftery, 'Iron-Age Ireland', in Ó Cróinín, *A New History of Ireland*, vol. 1 (Oxford, 2005), pp. 136–53, 180.

[8] *The Táin*, trans. T. Kinsella, with illustrations by Louis le Brocquy (Dublin, 1969).

CHAPTER TWO

The Saint Arrives

Golden grave goods, hearth stones from a Bronze Age fire, the remnants of old enclosures – these are the only remains of those early people who lived in east Cork and created the farmstead at Ballymaloe. The early farms of the Cloyne valley were just clearings in a dense forest of deciduous trees. The undergrowth was thick and the forest rich in wildlife: birds, deer and pigs, small rodents and insects. At first men made clearings and moved on, but as they became better farmers and the population increased, they began to settle. They spoke Gaelic and were part of small kingdoms which in turn had powerful overlords further north. It was the king in Cashel who sent St Colmán to Cloyne and altered the pattern of settlement so dramatically.

The fifth century in Ireland was one of startling change. Christianity and literacy both came into the country in that century, altering the culture radically. As they came at the same time, a whole world burst into life in the written records just as that world was about to change irrevocably. One of the early Christian teachers settled at Cloyne, and Ballymaloe, which was so close, became attached to his foundation.

First, let us locate Ballymaloe on the map of Gaelic Ireland. It was in Muma, now Munster, the southernmost province of the island. When Ireland burst through the veil of literacy, people were on the move, probably because the Roman Empire was collapsing, disrupting trade and power balances. Certainly, a new people was pushing into Munster from the north, the Eoganacht, who soon claimed over-lordship and made their capital at Cashel.

In the south-east older people were settled. Ballymaloe was within the kingdom of the Uí Liatháin with their principal fort at Castlelyons. One of the sons of the Uí Liatháin rulers held a sub-kingdom or fiefdom near the coast. His name was MacCaille and he gave his name to his small *tuatha* or kingdom. It was called

Uí MacCaille and is now the barony of Imokilly in which Ballymaloe lies.[1]

The people of the Cloyne valley probably never saw the new overlord who ruled from Cashel but it was he who made the decisive move. Coipre was the king at Cashel and he had a powerful *file*, Mac Léinín, meaning the son of Léinín, who was highly trained in Gaelic learning. A *file* was a poet, scholar and historian who memorised the history of the kingdom and composed poetry which was often in praise of the king and his warriors. The *file* acted as the memory of the tribe and as adviser to the king. He might have exceptional mental powers. This *file*, Mac Léinín, was so adept at the old ways that he was able to curse the king's enemies into submission.[2] Here was a man of ability; the king held him in high favour.

The old way of life among the Gaels had been one of conflict, sensuality and vibrant story-telling, with strong strains of magic. Gaelic society was laced with poetry and curses, taboos and obligations, all of great power. Warfare was endemic, a sort of competitive sport with consequences, which took up most of the summer. The annals make frequent reference to hostings when the warriors came together to feast, scheme and fight. So the extraordinary advent of Jesus' teaching which counselled peace and forgiveness could hardly have been more revolutionary. It came with prayer and written texts, mainly in Latin, which brought the world of Mediterranean culture into the fuming extravagances of the distant northern isle.

Christianity spread by transmission from teacher to pupil and Coipre's *file* learned the new teaching from Bréanainn of Clonfert. He converted to Christianity and took the name Colmán, meaning the dove – the dove of peace.

Colmán wanted to set up a Christian foundation and Coipre agreed, but he sent his *file* to the borders of his kingdom. He had recently established himself as overlord of the Uí Liatháin; the sub-kingdom of MacCaille had just been subjugated and the neighbouring tribes were not under Coipre's overlordship. Coipre sent Colmán to this recently conquered 'sword-land' to strengthen his presence there and to create a Christian foundation. The king gave Colmán an extensive grant of land and sent him south to Cloyne. The tribes would not dare attack a newly consecrated church which was set up by command of the king and under the law of sanctuary.[3]

---

[1] L. Ó Buachalla, 'Uí MacCaille in Pre-Norman Times', *Journal of the Cork Historical and Archaeological Society* (hereafter *JCHAS*), vol. L, 1945, p. 24.

[2] V. Hull, 'Conall Corc and the Corco Luigde', *PMLA* (Journal of the Modern Language Association of America), 1947, pp. 887–909.

[3] P. MacCotter, *Colmán of Cloyne: A Study* (Dublin, 2004), p. 38.

Early Christian Munster

A T L A N T I C

O C E A N

An Abhainn Mhór

Caisleán O Liatháin
Castlelyons

Lios Mór
Lismore

An Bhríd

Uí Liatháin

Uí Mictíre

Corcaigh
Cork

Little I.

MacTire's fortress
(Castlemartyr)

Uí MacCaille

Cluain Uamha
Cloyne

0   5   km 10

0   5   miles 10

Corco Duibne

C E L T

Map 3.

TVADMVMA

Lough
Derg

●Clonfertmulloe

AVRMVMA

Nore

Shannon

Eóganacht

●Cashel

Chaisil

Suir

ARMVMA

Déisi Mumuan

Blackwater

Uí Liatháin

●Lismore

Ardmore

Lee

Cork●

Castlemartyr
(MacTíre's fortress)

●Cloyne

★ BALLYMÁLOE

N

DESMVMA

Corco Lóigde

C   S   E   A

0   5   10   20   30   40   50 km

0   5   10   20   30   40   50 miles

So it was that Colmán and his followers arrived in the Cloyne valley, only a mile or so from Ballymaloe, to create a place of Christian worship. The tribesmen were not to molest the unusual new settlers but rather they were obliged to support the Christians with agricultural produce. The gift to Colmán was of fine land in an important position near the coast. For the Gaelic people of Imokilly it would gradually transform their society.

How startled they must have been in the nearby settlements. Many doubtless grumbled and we know some of the poets were furious at the new learning. Some may have threatened the monks, but the king had sent Colmán and slowly his foundation was accepted. Gaelic law was built on mutual obligation, so when Colmán and his followers offered teaching and sacred rites in return for dues in kind, the church began to fit into the existing system.[4]

Colmán spent his life at Cloyne, dying there in AD 600. He is said to have been buried in the graveyard at Cloyne, in the 'Fire House'. He became one of the early Irish saints but remained a poet who brought together the new skill of writing and native lore. Colmán lived at the crossroads of two ages, between pagan and Christian, and was influential in both. The saint was remembered long after his death as 'a man who loved poetry', and about twenty lines of verse remain which are thought to be his.[5]

When Colmán came to Cloyne, the people of Imokilly were farming and cattle herding, but Colmán's settlement influenced agricultural development. Christian devotion and steady work meant that monastic settlements grew into fine farms with advanced ideas in agriculture and medicine. Then they became places of healing and safety.

We know that several centuries later Ballymaloe was part of the Cloyne church lands and this seems to date from the early years of Colmán's foundation. Did Colmán's followers take over Ballymaloe or were the local farmers obliged to support the monastery and gradually drawn into its system? There is no way to answer that question and it was probably a little of both, but a medieval farm developed there which owed allegiance to the monastery. Church lands were often farmed by *manaig* families. These were married couples with children but they were also members of the monastery, so of intermediate status. The people at Ballymaloe in the early medieval years may well have been a *manaig* family.

There is another clue for thinking that, which is hidden in the name Ballymaloe, the farmstead of Mo-Lua. Mo-Lua is also the name of an early saint. St Mo-Lua came from what is now County Limerick and founded two religious houses, one at Clonfertmulloe. He lived in the early seventh century, so just after

---

4   D. Ó Cróinín, *A New History of Ireland*, vol. 1 (Oxford, 2005), p. 594.
5   P. Ó Riain, *A Dictionary of Irish Saints* (Dublin, 2001), pp. 185–6.

Colmán, and after his death Christians often took his name, as they did that of Patrick. Monks named Mo-Lua appear in the Annals of Inisfallen. The Mo-Lua who gave his name to the farm at Ballymaloe had the same name as this saint and was clearly a Christian.[6]

Foundations like Cloyne acted as *tuatha* or small kingdoms. The monastery owned land which was held by its own people. The name Mo-Lua probably dates from the early Christian era when the farm was in the gift of the Cloyne foundation and Mo-Lua settled there with his family. The name remains.

The monasteries prospered, influencing the secular population who learned from them and who often were dependent on them for skills and tools. It was often the monasteries that owned the local plough-team of oxen which all their tenants and dependants could use. The work would be shared among neighbouring farms attached to the mother church of Cloyne.

To imagine the farm at Ballymaloe in those early Christian centuries we can turn to the Irish law texts, which give a wealth of information from which historians have pieced together a full picture of farming in the seventh and eighth centuries. Dwellings then were built of timber and thatch and set within a wooden fence held by stone and earth foundations, often with a ditch outside. There are signs of such an enclosure in the field to the east of Ballymaloe House, but undated. Dwellings from this period were usually on higher ground for drainage and security.

By AD 800 farmsteads were home to an extended family of four generations, each adult male having his own arable land fenced off from his brothers'.[7] There would be several dwellings for the married couples and usually a separate cookhouse. The farmyard animals such as hens, dogs and often pigs were kept within the palisade where they were safe and could eat the scraps.

Cereal-growing increased in these centuries all over Ireland and the Cloyne valley had both a benign climate and good soil for grain. In many parts of Ireland wheat was a luxury but even before modern strains of wheat were developed, a crop could probably have been harvested at Ballymaloe. More common were barley and oats, for beer and porridge, although both crops were also used to make bread. Grinding corn was difficult. The farms had querns, two shaped stones ground against each other with a handle, but it was hard work; in aristocratic

---

[6] T.M. Charles-Edwards, *Early Christian Ireland* (Cambridge, 2000), pp. 2, 257; P. Ó Riain, *A Dictionary of Irish Saints* (Dublin, 2001), pp. 490–3; S. Mac Airt (ed.), *Annals of Inisfallen* (Dublin, 1977), entry for AD 743; Rev. J. Lanigan, *An Ecclesiastical History of Ireland*, vol. II, (Dublin, 1829), pp. 205–11; D.H. Farmer (ed.), *The Oxford Dictionary of Saints* (Oxford, 1979).

[7] Ó Cróinín, *A New History of Ireland*, p. 553.

households this work was done by female slaves and in lesser households by the wife and daughters. To reduce this labour and to produce better flour, watermills were developed and one of the earliest has been found on Little Island, in Cork harbour, which was in use by AD 630. Taking sacks of grain by horse and bringing back enough ground meal to feed the settlement at Ballymaloe would have been a big undertaking but there may have been a mill on the Womanagh River at Castlemartyr a little later. Watermills needed a strong flow of water; small streams were inadequate and in the summer even leats or larger rivers might not be strong enough. The farmer would hope for a dry harvest and the miller would hope for plentiful autumn rain as the farmers began to bring in their corn for grinding.

Cattle were important, central to Gaelic society and used to pay tribute, dowries and fines. They were kept for both meat and milk, as well as hides and fertiliser. Dairying became widespread from early Christian times; it suited Irish conditions and enormously improved the diet. There would have been a good cattle herd at Ballymaloe, probably taken up to higher ground in the summer, perhaps onto the ridge of hill to the north, in order to preserve the pasture in the valley.[8]

Sheep too were important, for wool as much as for their meat. They seem to have been the preserve of women; according to Gaelic law texts, a woman claiming an inheritance of land had to enter it accompanied by ewes.[9] There had been horses in Ireland for centuries but they were generally owned by people of status and used for riding rather than farm-work. Horse racing was popular; perhaps a few local horses went down to the beach for a race at low tide.

Apart from ploughing, the farm-work was done by spade or hand tools, and was hard. Slavery continued in Ireland until the twelfth century but the Church of Patrick frowned on it and slavery must have died out around Cloyne. On a substantial farm like Ballymaloe there would be labourers and servants who performed the heaviest part of the constant physical work. Bringing in wood, stoking fires, preparing food, drawing water, managing livestock, ploughing, weeding and harvesting, mending tools and buildings – there was constant physical activity.

In 707 Cloyne became an abbey, taking on new rules and status. The Irish Church had developed high levels of scholarship which were influential throughout Christian Europe. There was a library and a law school at Cloyne. The family at Ballymaloe might lead an agricultural life of hard work but good diet, while just along the old trackway was a religious foundation of great significance.

---

8   F. Mitchell and M. Ryan, *Reading the Irish Landscape* (Dublin, 1997), p. 249.

9   F. Kelly, *Early Irish Farming* (Dublin, 2001), p. 67.

The Abbot of Cloyne had influence over a wide area, while monks and scholars would visit Cloyne to study. The monks, in their robes with crosses on their chests and the long hoods which they pulled up in wet weather, must have been a familiar sight as they came and went through Imokilly. The Ballymaloe family would go to services at the abbey church and bury their dead in the graveyard. For over three centuries Ireland was one of the flowers of Christendom but as before, new people were about to thrust themselves into the life of Imokilly.

CHAPTER THREE

Invaders

Ballymaloe is in the parish of Kilmahon. The parishes took their form later, but many of the little country churches date from those early centuries. The church of Kilmahon is dedicated to an early sixth-century Gaelic woman and may give a tiny clue about life at Ballymaloe in those early Christian days.

Beside the marshy shoreline at Shanagarry the old graveyard of Kilmahon is all that remains of a once-living church which has twice become ruined, but keeps alive the name of a saint. Kilmahon is the church of Mahon or Macha who was one of Colmán's five sisters, all of whom were influential in the early Irish Church. At Killiney on the coast south of Dublin, a sixth-century church was dedicated to them. It seems that Mahon came to Cloyne with her brother; the townland of Kilva north-west of Cloyne was named for her[1] and there was a legend that St Colmán threw a stone at his sister at Geara near Ballinacurra which suggests she was actually with him in Imokilly. The remnants of a church and the graveyard beside the sea at Kilmahon may have been a settlement for early Christian women founded by the saint's sister.[2]

The old trackways which grew into roads have probably not changed that much; the road from Cloyne to Kilmahon goes past the entrance to Ballymaloe. Is it fanciful to think that the brother and sister walked that way in those early days or rode on horses since they were a family of status in Gaelic Christian society?

As the new religion spread, the settlements of the first teachers took on new roles. If Mahon lived at Shanagarry, her sanctuary became a little church. The local people had duties and obligations to their parish church, for example if a

---

[1] Originally Kilmawe. See E. St J. Brooks, 'Unpublished Charters Relating to Ireland, 1177–82, from the Archives of the City of Exeter', *Proceedings of the Royal Irish Academy*, section C, vol. 43, 1935–7, p. 348.

[2] Ibid.; P. MacCotter, *Colmán of Cloyne: A Study* (Dublin, 2004), p. 126; M. Brady, *Clerical and Parochial Records of Cork, Cloyne and Ross*, vol. II (London, 1863), pp. 278–9.

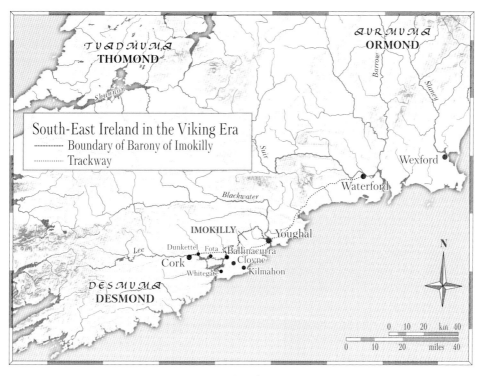

Map 4.

Gaelic woman married outside her parish she still paid dues to her natal church.[3] Ballymaloe may have been linked to Kilmahon from early on and owed the church produce or service, given for the parish priest who ran that church and who guided the people clustered around it on the coast.

The image we have of Ireland in the first three centuries of Christianity is of an island developing quickly, blessed with ample food supplies where learning grew and society was stable. The monasteries became powerful institutions creating development, and so it was at Cloyne. Once it became an abbey, the abbot was a significant man with a large landed estate and wide pastoral duties.

Ballymaloe was not just part of that estate but very close to the mother church and the town which grew up around it. Ballymaloe was *termann* or church lands; it was part of the kingdom of the abbot who held the lands of the founder as if in trust. But monasteries were also collegiate and the family at Ballymaloe had a place and a role in that great brotherhood. *Manaig* families were educated by the monastic teachers and some had voting rights when it came to selecting a new

---

[3] D. Ó Corráin, 'Ireland c. 800: Aspects of Society', in D. Ó Cróinín, *A New History of Ireland*, vol. 1 (Oxford, 2005), p. 597.

abbot. In times of strife they might be called upon to fight.[4] Under church rules, they could marry but there were restrictions on their sexual activity, which gave them a mixed status, neither as pure as celibate monks nor yet rustic sinners of the general kind. Within the abbeys there were areas of true holiness with less sacred outer precincts; who could enter the various areas depended on their level of sinfulness, so the *manaig* families were partial insiders.[5]

It was a society with cultural riches and vibrant religion, but strangers appeared in the eighth century who cared nothing for either. Ballymaloe was sheltering under the protection of the abbey in Cloyne when the first Viking raids on Ireland began. The Norsemen came in long ships and pushed into river mouths, plundering abbeys for their fine vessels and artefacts. They were in Cork in 822 and in the Blackwater in 833, raiding Lismore. News of their ferocity spread; Cloyne was vulnerable. Then the Norsemen began to stay over winter and built forts for their ships as way-stations on their long journeys. The first recorded attack on Cloyne was in 888 when the deputy abbot was killed. Ballymaloe, so close to the abbey, was vulnerable during raids on Cloyne and the men there could be called on to defend the church.

To prepare for attack a round tower was constructed. They were being built elsewhere at the time and Cloyne thought one necessary. From the top a lookout could see down to the coast and a bell high in the tower would be heard far away. From Ballymaloe the sound of the bell would have rung out across the fields and treetops from the nearby town, warning people and calling the men for defence. People could hurry to the abbey for protection or gather behind palisades to ward off attack.

Gradually the Norsemen attacked less and traded more. They built settlements in the best harbours and slowly some became Christian. There was intermarriage and even close to Ballymaloe some Viking settlement: at Fota and Whitegate. Their strange language became familiar and their trade goods popular. Gaelic Ireland had modest overseas trade, mainly to Britain, but the Scandinavians were international merchants with trade networks extending across Europe and into Asia. Tall, strong and weather-beaten from their sea voyages, they brought new goods and styles to Ireland; amber from the Baltic, silver from Russia, combs and brooches, exotic spices from Asia.[6] Perhaps for the first time, pepper, cinnamon

---

[4]   K. Hughes, 'The Church in Irish Society, 400–800', in Ó Cróinín, *A New History of Ireland*, pp. 312–17.

[5]   Ó Corráin, 'Ireland c. 800: Aspects of Society', in Ó Cróinín, *A New History of Ireland*, p. 598.

[6]   P. Sawyer (ed.), *Oxford Illustrated History of the Vikings* (Oxford, 1997); D. Ó Cróinín, *Early Medieval Ireland, 400–1200* (London, 1995), pp. 234–50.

and other oriental spices were tested in the cooking pots of Ballymaloe. The Vikings minted coins in Dublin, which altered commerce, and they had all sorts of tempting objects. The abbot might frown and fathers warn, but doubtless there were girls at Ballymaloe who lingered a little to talk to the tall strangers and hoped for some delicious hair ornament from the east brought by the tall strangers with their mastery of the sea.

Despite all these changes the ruling dynasties of the area had continued, but rivalries and warfare increased as new families became dominant. Munster was divided; the O'Briens ruled Thomond in the north and west, the MacCarthys holding Desmond (Deas Muma) in the south. Imokilly was contested territory. Cloyne was attacked by men from Leinster in 978 and a century later Diarmit O'Brien came by sea and plundered Cloyne.[7] In 1137 all the early buildings at Cloyne were burned.[8] But the abbey at Cloyne always emerged from these attacks and continued. In fact, in 1152 it was elevated to a diocese, giving it a bishop who ruled a large area. This would have important consequences for Ballymaloe.

During this century the parish boundaries were more formally organised. Maps show the long finger of land from which tithes would now have to be paid to Kilmahon. The old obligation had become a feudal tax.

Then the Normans arrived and warfare intensified. When Henry II of England came to claim over-lordship of Ireland, he gave three *tuatha* to the east of Cork to his knight Robert FitzStephen. This included the barony of Imokilly in which stood Ballymaloe.

The local ruler put up a strong fight. Mac Tíre had his stronghold on the trackway from Youghal to Cork, near where Castlemartyr now stands. In 1189 'a great slaughter was inflicted on the foreigners' and the Cloyne area was devastated by war. Mac Tíre arranged an ambush in which all the leading Normans of eastern Cork were killed, including FitzStephen's son. At this, the Irish all over Desmond rose and Imokilly was engulfed by war. Despite smaller numbers, the Normans had far superior weapons which the courage and daring of the Irish could not match. The Normans gained control.

Because FitzStephen's son was dead, his cousins inherited the grants of land in east Cork. Descended from Gerald of Windsor and a Welsh princess, they knew Gaelic ways but they were tough, ambitious Norman fighters. Maurice FitzGerald and Philip de Barry could lay claim to three fine *tuatha* or baronies to the east of Cork.[9]

---

[7] S. Mac Airt (ed.), *Annals of Inisfallen* (Dublin, 1977), p. 241.

[8] 'Cloyne', in *Encyclopedia of Ireland* (Dublin, 1968).

[9] G.H. Orpen, *Ireland under the Normans, 1169–1333* (Dublin, 2005), pp. 163–8.

The Irish family at Ballymaloe must have been fearful. The Normans were Christian and respected the Church, but they had a different legal system to the Irish and they were entrepreneurs, hungry for land and the profits to be made from it. They would soon cast their sharp eyes over the fine fields at Ballymaloe.

The land ownership records are sparse for the thirteenth century but sure enough, when Ballymaloe next appears in the records the owner has a French name.

CHAPTER FOUR

Norman Settlers at Ballymaloe

Despite resistance from local Irish rulers, the Normans quickly gained control of east Cork. The Church however was sacrosanct, which gave protection to the clergy and tenants. But Henry II had a grant of Ireland from the pope and claimed rights over the Irish Church too.[1] Gradually the Irish family at Ballymaloe became vulnerable. By physical might and by law the fine farms of the Cloyne valley were soon in Norman hands.

First they took the walled ports of Waterford, Youghal and Cork. Then they built fortresses on the highway at Castlemartyr and Ballinacurra.[2] But the Church lands were in the gift of the bishop, who was Irish, ruling through his Irish dean and chapter. As early as 1226 the king demanded an English bishop at Cloyne but the chapter resisted and it was 1284 before a native Englishman was appointed.[3] Once the bishop was English, the Church lands fell under English control. The Irish Church with its network of families was broken up and the feudal system of manors was instigated with the bishop as Lord of Cloyne. Ballymaloe became a feudal holding and its Irish owners lost possession.[4]

The old kings had taken tribute; the English one was efficient at making inventories leading to taxation. In 1301 a justiciar came on circuit to Cork and stayed for fifteen days valuing land for tax. Ballymelyn is how he spelled

1   G.L. Hand, *English Law in Ireland, 1290–1324* (Cambridge, 1967), p. 176.
2   J.T. Collins, 'Ui Mac Caille, AD 177 to 1700', *JCHAS*, vol. L, 1945, pp. 31–9; S. Mac Airt (ed.), *Annals of Inisfallen* (Dublin, 1977), entry for AD 1206; G.H. Orpen, *Ireland under the Normans, 1169–1333* (Dublin, 2005), p. 168.
3   J. Ware, *Works* (Dublin, 1736), pp. 574–8; Brady, *Clerical and Parochial Records of Cork, Cloyne and Ross,* vol. III (London, 1863–1864), pp. 92–6.
4   Hand, *English Law in Ireland*, Chapter X.

Ballymaloe.[5] He did not list the owners but we know who had taken possession because three years later Elisa le Blund made a legal claim on behalf of her son. Her husband Philip le Blund had been serjeant at McKill, north of Fermoy, and after his death his widow applied for formal custody of their son Simon, and for confirmation of his inheritance. This was Ballymaloe and six other land-holdings. Ballymaloe had two carucates of land and so it was a large farm – one carucate was the amount of land that a team of eight oxen could till in a single growing season, reckoned to be 120 acres depending on the land. Ballymaloe then was a farm of about 240 acres, much the same size as it was centuries later. Simon was a boy when he inherited but he had a good estate, with 100 acres at Rathcoursey and other smaller holdings. Big landowners often had large and scattered estates from which they collected dues but seldom saw. However, Ballymaloe was Simon's main inheritance in Imokilly so he and his widowed mother probably lived there.

Simon le Blund held Ballymaloe from John le Poer, who was lord of the manor of Shanagarry, part of the large manor of Inchiquin established near Youghal. In the early phase of Norman expansion the invaders had extended their influence outwards from the major ports, and the manor of Inchiquin, although it was not one tract of land, had encroached on the lands of Cloyne cathedral.[6]

The le Blunds soon became influential in Cloyne. Once an Englishman was established as bishop, it soon followed that an Englishman was appointed dean. This was an influential position as the dean was the head of the chapter and managed the landed estate belonging to Cloyne cathedral. John le Blond's appointment in 1324 gave him a key role at the cathedral.[7]

The le Blund or le Blond family had been in Ireland since the Norman invasion. The earliest le Blund was related to Earl Hugh de Lacy, who was a favourite of Henry II. Walter le Blund was sent to Ulster soon after the invasion, where he was awarded a large estate. Le Blund means 'fair', and as the Normans anglicised their names, the family became known as Whyte or White. A Walter le Whyt joined the Bruce invasion of Ireland in 1315 and was subsequently exiled. There were other Whytes in Munster; a Robert White was mayor of Limerick in 1213 and they held influential positions in Clonmel and Tipperary.[8]

---

[5] L. Ó Buachalla, 'An Early Fourteenth-Century Placename List for Anglo-Norman Cork', *Dinnseanchas* II, nos 1 & 2, 1966, p. 44.

[6] P. MacCotter and K. Nicholls (eds), *The Pipe Roll of Cloyne* (Midleton, 1996), pp. 169–70; A. O'Brien, 'The Settlement of Imokilly and the Formation and Descent of the Manor of Inchiquin', *JCHAS*, vol. 87, 1982, pp. 21–6.

[7] Brady, *Clerical and Parochial,* vol. II, p. 196.

[8] Orpen, *Ireland under the Normans,* pp. 168, 530; B. Burke, *Burke's Irish Family Records,* White of Tipperary (Buckingham, 2007).

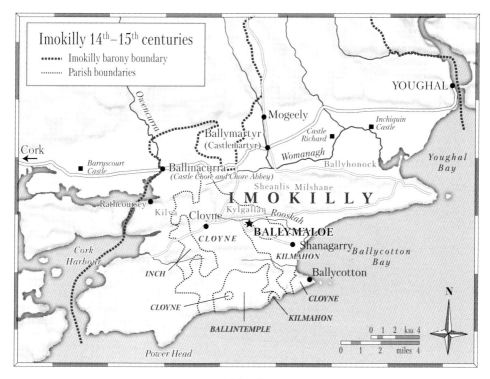

Map 5.

The property at Ballymaloe was a substantial holding on good land; much of it seems to have been arable. Living on the land with small dwellings and plots of their own would be a workforce, most of them Irish. People were moving into the area from Britain, especially from the West Country of England, but few of them brought labourers or villeins to till the land. Irish society had been highly stratified; now under the Normans the unfree Irish became agricultural labourers in the Irish version of the feudal system and were known as *betaghs*.[9] Some higher-status Irish got rights under English law and some took English names, but many moved west into areas still controlled by Irish leaders and their law. We have no record of the Irish owners of Ballymaloe at the time of the conquest, nor of what happened to them.

The local language of administration and commerce became English. As to the building that Simon le Blund lived in, the Normans used structures not unlike the palisaded farmsteads of the Irish but with stronger defences. Their great fortresses were stone-built and massive, but the smaller castles and farmsteads such as

9   J. Otway-Ruthven, 'The Native Irish and English Law in Medieval Ireland', *Irish Historical Studies*, vol. 7, no. 25, 1950, pp. 1–16.

Ballymaloe were much like the Irish ones, timber-built dwellings surrounded by a fence. The Normans however dug ditches and used the earth to raise mounds at one end of the dwelling area to make a more defensible structure. Both the Irish and the Normans created defensive structures on cliffs and outcrops, so the dwellings at Ballymaloe were probably already sited on the rocky outcrop where they now stand. However, the Normans had much better tools and brought into Ireland their techniques for building in stone. At first only the Crown built stone fortresses but as time went on stone was used for domestic buildings too. The earliest stone structure still standing at Ballymaloe is the tower, now embedded in the west end of the house. There may be archaeological remains underneath the current house or elsewhere on the farm which are earlier but the stone structures now standing at Ballymaloe House date from several centuries after the Norman invasion.[10]

Land was held by feudal tenure and more details are given in a comprehensive list made by the cathedral authorities in 1364. Simon le Blund must have died by this time but his family were still at Ballymaloe. A new bishop had arrived the previous year, John de Swaffham, a native of Norfolk. He demanded an inventory of his estates. There had been changes in tenants and in their tenure over the years; the records were not complete and the bishop instructed his officials to make a thorough valuation. The portreeve, who was the chief officer of the manor, was responsible for collecting the rents and keeping the accounts. He was elected annually and led the corporation, which consisted of twelve free burgesses. The enquiry was held at the manor court in Cloyne Castle with a jury to confirm the details. Cloyne cathedral had a substantial landed estate and each holding was recorded with the tenants and the dues that each paid.[11]

Scribes wrote the valuation out on ten parchment membranes, later sewed together as a list – the Pipe Roll of Cloyne. The estate still reflected the first gift of land given to St Colmán, for it included the lands he had been given in north Cork as well as those around Cloyne; all were listed among the possessions of the see. The Pipe Roll started with the big holdings near the town which paid cash and service rents; among these was Ballymaloe. It then continued through the

---

[10] D. Power (comp.), *Archaeological Inventory of Cork. Vol. 2: East and South Cork* (Dublin, 1994), no. 5432; H. Leask, *Irish Castles and Castellated Houses* (Dundalk, 1995); T. O'Keefe, 'The Archaeology of Norman Castles in Ireland: Part 1: Mottes and Ringworks', *Archaeology Ireland*, vol. 4, no. 3, 1990, pp. 15–17; C.T. Donnelly, 'Frowning Ruins: The Tower Houses of Medieval Ireland', *History Ireland*, vol. 4, no. 1, 1996, pp. 11–16.

[11] R. Caulfield (transcribed and with an introduction by), *Rotulus Pipæ Clonensis* (Cork, 1859).

small burgage tenants in Cloyne, to the fishermen of Ballycotton who paid in fish.

Of Ballymaloe, the Pipe Roll states that:

> Richard Whyte holds of the lord, Kylgallan which lies beside the burgagery of Cloyne on the west, and Balymoloye, and [he holds] by homage, fealty, wardship, knight's service, common suit of court, and by the service of 5s. yearly at the usual terms.[12]

The le Blund family had become Whyte. They held Ballymaloe as feudal tenants owing money rent and were due for military service should the lord bishop demand it. Kylgallan was slightly nearer the town.

There were other Whytes in Imokilly; the family were not great magnates but they were substantial land-holders. The family at Ballymaloe had cousins at Mogeely, a property they had bought from the Carews. The Mogeely Whytes stayed at Crowbally for centuries and will come into our story again later on.

The Whytes no longer held Ballymaloe from the le Poers but directly from the lord – the bishop of Cloyne. There had been a contest over Church lands in east Cork which the bishop had won. The Church had asserted its rights in the manor of Inchiquin, and Ballymaloe had come back into the estate of the Church. The holder of Shanagarry was now a tenant of the Church and paying dues to the bishop.[13]

Cloyne had altered dramatically. The landowners and officials spoke English, while law was in Latin; only the *betaghs* and Irish artisans spoke Gaelic as their first language. Sometime in the thirteenth century a new stone nave had been built which grew to become the cathedral church. This new cathedral was the core of a bustling feudal borough, a status which helped to promote commerce. Cloyne, then and now, had two streets which crossed at the centre, known as Irish (north–south) and English (east–west) Streets. All the church buildings were in the south-east quarter of the town, with the cathedral and graveyard at the lower end of Irish Street and the bishop's castle in the same quarter but nearer the crossroads. The castle had been recently built and stood among gardens and grounds with an entrance onto the street leading to the cathedral.[14] It was known as Cloyne Castle or Cross Castle. The manor court was held here, rents and feudal dues were paid and the business of the diocese conducted. When Richard

12 MacCotter and Nicholls, *The Pipe Roll of Cloyne*, pp. 10–11.
13 O'Brien, 'The Settlement of Imokilly', pp. 21–6.
14 H. Lynch, 'The Bishop's Palace' in P. Ó Loingsigh (ed.), *The Book of Cloyne* (Midleton, 1994), p. 139.

Whyte had to pay his rent or attend the manor court it was to the bishop's office in Cloyne that he came. It was in this castle that the inquisition was held into the bishop's lands which led to the Pipe Roll of Cloyne.

Old texts refer to the 'land of peace' created after the Norman invasion where local warfare ceased and prosperity increased. The Normans achieved their aims quickly. By Richard Whyte's time, the population had grown, productivity had risen and exports from the area had greatly increased; wool, hides, cloth and furs were going out from the ports in good quantities, repaying the conquest and its military commitment. The thirteenth century had been a time of tremendous development and doubtless Ballymaloe was being farmed more intensively.

But by the time the Pipe Roll was written up in the fourteenth century, conditions were deteriorating. The Bruce invasion of 1315, a deteriorating climate and then the Black Death were all weakening the English lordship. The Irish were restive and breaking into the English areas from the west. Some settlers left for England and everywhere the control of the central authority was breaking down. As a result, local magnates took on greater power and the Crown – in danger of losing control in Ireland completely – promoted the leading families to rule under royal authority in their local areas. This brought the FitzGeralds back into prominence in Imokilly and before long they were at Ballymaloe.

CHAPTER FIVE

The Seneschal and the Dean

The Whites held Ballymaloe by feudal service from the bishop of Cloyne for about two centuries, yet we have little record of their lives there. They also had Kylgallan which was just west of Ballymaloe, nearer Cloyne. In the early seventeenth century, Nicholas White still had Kylgallan but Ballymaloe had passed out of his hands and become a FitzGerald property.[1]

This may have happened legally and naturally, but not all of the FitzGeralds' transactions were either legal or natural, so we cannot be sure how Ballymaloe was acquired. In the fifteenth century, a branch of the FitzGerald family began to assert domination over much of Imokilly. The reason for this was not the ancient grant from invasion times but the breakdown of law and order. As the ascent of the Imokilly FitzGeralds is crucial to Ballymaloe's story, we must first trace their extraordinary rise in east Cork.

They had come as conquerors, these descendants of Gerald who traced their line back to an Italian magnate. Gerald's father had come to England with William the Conqueror, Gerald was among the men sent to take and hold Wales, becoming constable of Pembroke Castle, and Gerald's grandsons crossed the Irish Sea to make Ireland a possession of the Crown of England. Yet over two centuries the FitzGeralds became Gaelicised, especially the Earls of Desmond who settled on the mouth of the Shannon in western Munster. It was this line which became so powerful in Imokilly.

Their rise in east Cork was the result of the weakening of the English lordship in late medieval times. The Earl of Desmond was the head of the FitzGeralds in Munster and had a great fiefdom based around the Shannon estuary but stretching right across Munster. In 1420 he was appointed as seneschal – or sheriff – of Imokilly and he in turn sent his kinsman Richard, the illegitimate son of the

---

[1] R. Caulfield, *The Council Book of the Corporation of Youghal* (Guildford, 1878), Appendix D, p. 585.

Knight of Kerry, to take up the position. Richard probably arrived in Imokilly in 1422 and was given a property on the Womanagh River where he built Castle Richard, which stayed in his family after they got a larger headquarters. Richard was the first of seven seneschals, a job inherited by the eldest son until rebellion and war ended their rule. Richard had six sons, all of whom were given fine properties in Imokilly.[2]

The seneschal was the principal law officer of the barony. The local people said he was not just judge, but 'judge, jury, gallows, rope and all'. He was not only seneschal but captain of the kern, or foot soldiers. He and his descendants earned the nickname *Madraí na Fola* – the dogs of blood.

Maurice, the second seneschal, moved to the old headquarters of the barony, on the highway at Ballymartyr, where he constructed a fortress known as the Castle of Imokilly from which he ruled and which became Castlemartyr. His brothers' lands were nearby or nearer to Youghal. With central government so weak there was little to stop them pursuing their ambitions for land and wealth, except that so much of Imokilly belonged to the Church.

It was not surprising then that Richard the seneschal's descendants took up clerical jobs. At the time the See of Cloyne had been joined to that of Cork. The bishop lived in the city, so Cloyne Castle was only used for administration, which was managed by the dean. As the bishop was an enormous landowner and his position so influential, all the leading families were keen to get hold of the bishopric; a Roche, a MacCarthy and a FitzGerald all competed for it at the same time.[3]

Gerald FitzGerald, son of the first seneschal, was working as a clerk in the Bishop's Palace in Cork and conceived, with the connivance of Roche and the archdeacon, an audacious plan. Gerald forged papers stating that Bishop Jordan was too infirm to carry on and had resigned his see. By sending these to Rome, Gerald and his accomplices gained control first of the lands and then of the actual bishopric. When Bishop Jordan discovered that he was being deprived, he remonstrated and wrote to both the king and the pope. Gerald was ejected – but he still became bishop after Jordan's death.[4]

Three of the first seneschal's descendants became bishop in turn. This allowed

---

2   Ibid., pp. xii–xiii; T.C. Croker, *Researches in the South of Ireland* (London, 1824), p. 239.

3   See P. MacCotter, 'The Geraldine Clerical Lineages of Imokilly', in D. Edwards, *Regions and Rulers in Ireland, 1100–1650* (Dublin, 2004), pp. 54–78; Brady, *Clerical and Parochial*, vol. III, pp. 42–3.

4   Brady, *Clerical and Parochial*, vol. III, pp. 42–3.

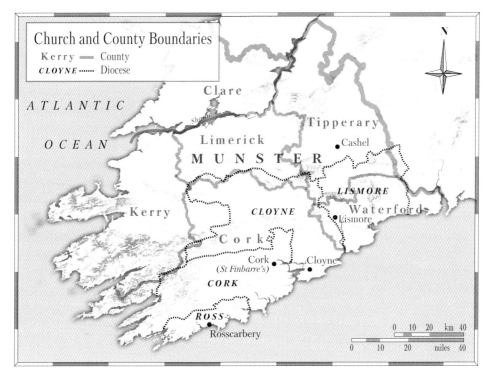

Map 6.

them to appoint their relatives to the churches of the diocese and so benefit from the glebe lands and tithes. The third Geraldine bishop was John, who held the see from 1499 to 1520, but after his death the family conceived a simple and practical strategy. The dean managed the Church lands of Cloyne and was based in the town. If one of the family became dean, they could manage the whole estate to their advantage. Not long afterwards the position became vacant and David FitzJames of the Castle Richard Geraldines became Dean of Cloyne.[5] The family

---

[5]   Fitz means son of: the FitzGeralds were the descendants of Gerald of Windsor. Throughout this period the men of the family were known by their own and their father's name. For example David son of James was called David FitzJames. In written records this might be written various ways: David FitzJames Gerald, David FitzJames FitzGerald or David FitzJames fitz Gerald. The family collectively were known as the FitzGeralds or as the Geraldines. As regards the form I will use in this account, quotations will be as in the original documents, I will omit the father's name, and the family name will be written FitzGerald. However, the last dean was generally known as John FitzEdmund without a family name and this is a form I will also use. James FitzMaurice was frequently known simply as FitzMaurice and was famous under that name which will be retained.

held this position for four generations, culminating with the extraordinary life of John FitzEdmund FitzGerald of Ballymaloe.[6]

The job of dean gave them control over the see lands as well as over the cathedral. They also managed the bishop's castle in the town, known as Cloyne Castle, which stood in its own grounds near the crossroads.[7] Here the Church officials, headed by the dean, managed the running of the cathedral and all the issues arising from a large landed estate. The FitzGeralds held this position for almost a century. They must have been familiar figures in the town with its ancient tower and medieval buildings. 'The Dean' became the title by which several members of the family were known, as they swept into the old castle in their official gowns clutching their rolls of parchment. Men came in to see them about land matters, rental payments and boundary disputes, water courses and legal issues. The See of Cloyne owned several good houses in town in which the dean may have lived, until they became bold in their new position and settled themselves in the bishop's castle.

While the younger branch was becoming established as managers of the Church lands, the seneschals had developed their role too. By the use of feudal claims of one sort of another, the seneschal was collecting dues from almost every land-holder in Imokilly in Tudor times.[8] But that was a period of immense change; fateful choices would have to be made.

At Ballymaloe, as on many other land-holdings, there had been substantial building. In 1429 a law was passed in Dublin which gave a grant of £10 to every man in the Pale who built a castle within ten years, stipulating the minimum dimensions it should be. Landowners are never slow to claim government grants so a spate of building began around Dublin which spread down the east coast of Ireland.[9] Landowners who were nervous about increasing lawlessness, keen to follow the trend or to pick up a government grant got busy building.

The tower which now exists at Ballymaloe is the turret of a larger castle or tower house which was built on the strata of rock where it emerged above the surface of the land. The siting was precise, on a rocky outcrop beside a steep drop and a reliable well. With the Rooskah River to the rear and the flat fields to the front, the landholder built a stone castle out of local limestone. Tower houses are a development of the earlier defended settlements, but now they were protected

---

[6] Brady, *Clerical and Parochial,* vol. II, p. 196; H. Cotton, *Fasti Ecclesiae Hibernicae*, vol. I (Dublin, 1846–1878), p. 310.

[7] H.T. Fleming, 'Some of the History of the Castell and See Demesne of Cloyne', *JCHAS*, 2nd ser. vol. IX, no. 60, 1896, pp. 209–23.

[8] Caulfield, *Council Book Youghal*, Appendix C.

[9] D. Sweetman, *The Medieval Castles of Ireland* (Cork, 2005), p. 137.

6.   *West end of Ballymaloe House showing the turret.*

within a stone wall which enclosed the tower and an open domestic space, the bawn. Often there was a single-storey hall within the bawn where business was transacted and retainers gathered. The living quarters of the family were within the tower house.

The existing structure at Ballymaloe is a corner turret which was attached to the larger stone structure. Inside the turret there is a staircase and small chambers, with slit windows for light, air and defence. The stairway originally rose further than the current roof, suggesting there was another floor. Two doorways open out of the turret into a structure that was once the main part of the castle but which no longer exists. It would have been a castle similar to nearby Castle Richard – built by the seneschal – or to Barryscourt near Carrigtohill which belonged to the Barry family and is still intact. Both these latter castles were built for leading feudal families with military duties, unlike Ballymaloe which was therefore not as substantial. Without excavations the size and layout can only be surmised, but we can be fairly sure of the ground plan. To east and west there are the remains of stout walls which were once the old bawn walls. At the turret end they are battered at the base, showing their origins. At the rear the bawn wall was built on the rock at the edge of the valley so only the front or south part of the wall has been lost and covered over, but the paved terrace roughly covers the site of the late medieval bawn.[10]

The building of the tower house altered the way of life of the family. In the earlier settlement there were a variety of structures and the cookhouse was often separate. Some late medieval castles still had a separate kitchen as cooking was messy and fire a hazard, but the tower house was a sophisticated structure and often had a kitchen in the basement or on the ground floor. The first floor frequently had a reception room with large fireplace but the hall – as a space for business and the gathering of men – became separated out from family life in the tower. On the upper floor of the tower house and in the turret chambers, members of the family could sleep or withdraw to a warmer private space.

The tower house and an open space outside it were contained within the bawn wall, creating a courtyard in which servants did the housework, men would gather for defence, horses could be kept safely, smaller livestock might be reared and where the messier household chores of firewood and food preparation could be carried out. Contained within its defensive wall, this is where the family and their retainers would gather when the castle was under attack.

On the north side, the bawn wall was long and straight. It rose from the rocky outcrop, giving the castle an even more secure position with the drop to the valley of the Rooskah below. This long, straight wall was the key structure and is still the spine of the current house. At one end was the existing turret, with probably another at the other end where there was an opening in the wall which led to the well. There may have been other turrets to the south at the corners of the bawn wall and possibly one to the north to strengthen the wall on the river side, but if so, nothing remains of them.

The spine wall on the lip of the valley remained the defining structure of the house throughout all the subsequent phases of building. Fireplaces were built onto it and floor timbers attached to it. The house has been extended and rebuilt several times, so few of the fifteenth- or sixteenth-century structures are intact; only the turret and the spine wall remain from that time.[11]

Central to the tower house were its chimneys. Often the main reception room was on the first floor and shared a chimney with the kitchen below. Meat, grain,

---

[10] Frank Keohane, Professor Tadhg O'Keeffe and Jeremy Williams all contributed their expertise regarding the layout and development of Ballymaloe House.

[11] D. Power (comp.), *Archaeological Inventory of Cork, vol. 2: East and South Cork* (Dublin, 1994), p. 220. The classic work on castles is H. Leask, *Irish Castles and Castellated Houses* (Dundalk, 1995); R. Sherlock, 'The Evolution of the Irish Tower-house as a Domestic Space', *Proceedings of the Royal Irish Academy*, vol. 111C, 2010; T. O'Keeffe, *Medieval Irish Buildings, 1100–1600* (Dublin, 2015).

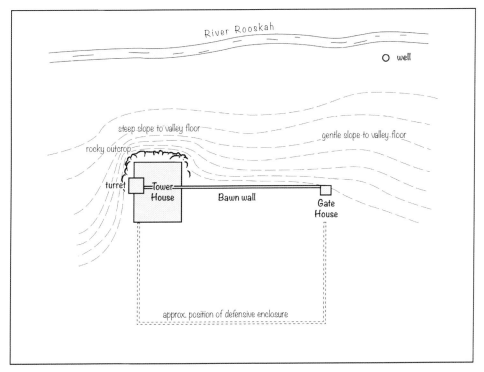

Plan 1.　The tower house, 15th – 16th century.

vegetables and milk were brought in from the farm for preparation within the bawn. Water was carried in from the well, making the entrance beside the river essential but giving the castle a slight weakness there if attacked. Although no farm buildings have survived from this period, they were probably on the same site as the current farmyard where there would be fodder for horses and most of the livestock would be kept. When people left the castle they could either cross the Rooskah and ride up the track to the north leading towards Castlemartyr or turn right and cross the meadow eastwards to the coast or westwards to the Cloyne road.

It is generally believed that the FitzGeralds built the tower house but it is possible that the Whites were still there until the sixteenth century. Some branch of the FitzGeralds are said to have got possession of it before the most notorious of the deans moved in during the 1580s. Ballymaloe was not among the properties which the first seneschal gave to his sons, although neighbouring Barnabrow was.[12] A junior branch of the FitzGeralds at nearby Milshane and

---

[12] Caulfield, *Council Book Youghal*, pp. x–xi.

Sheanlis may have acquired Ballymaloe.[13] Since the Geraldines had large families of sons, within a generation or two of arriving in Imokilly they were settled on many of the finest holdings in the barony, but there is no firm record of them at Ballymaloe until the late sixteenth century.

So it is possible that the Whites built the tower house, but if so they did not keep it for long. It is far more likely that the FitzGeralds built it, as even the junior branches were prospering and acquiring property. The Whites had certainly lost Ballymaloe by Elizabeth I's reign, but at Mogeely the White family prospered and across the barony Whites had substantial holdings in the early seventeenth century. So it was not family decline which removed them from Ballymaloe. The FitzGeralds found a way to remove them from a choice property near the town.

For the FitzGeralds this was a time of swift advance. The first FitzGerald to become dean was David, who was descended from the junior branch of the seneschal's family at Castle Richard. He was followed by James, who was born in the late fifteenth century as Henry VII was establishing himself as the first Tudor monarch, a dynasty of modernisers and centralisers who instigated the Reformation.

By the time James FitzGerald became dean in 1535, the crucial legislation had been passed in England to cement Henry VIII's break with Rome. By then the Imokilly FitzGeralds were well-thought-of in London. A warrant was signed by Henry VIII in the same year ordering that Master Edmund, the nephew of James, Dean of Cloyne, was to have the bishopric. Although he was never installed, the family were clearly in favour with the Crown. By then new Tudor administrators were arriving to bring Ireland into line with the English system and the deans had apparently made a good impression on them. In Dublin, a parliament was called to legislate for reformation in both the Irish Church and state.

When Henry VIII decided to break from Rome, choices had to be made and the dean's family decided to support the Crown. When James died, his son Edmund (Edmund FitzJames) became Dean of Cloyne and was among those who agreed to 'annihilate the usurped authority of the bishop of Rome' and to support the authority of the bishops appointed by King Henry.[14] The rift with Rome had been accomplished and the FitzGerald deans had declared their support.

Edmund became the dean soon after the break with Rome and held the post for over twenty years. He had property and the benefit of several Church livings. Edmund lived a full life, marrying three times as well as siring children by his

---

[13]   P. MacCotter and K. Nicholls (eds.), *The Pipe Roll of Cloyne* (Midleton, 1996), pp. 154–5.
[14]   MacCotter, 'The Geraldine Clerical Lineages of Imokilly', p. 65.

mistress Honor Ní Donogh from west Cork, who was mother to his eldest son.[15] In all, Dean Edmund had nine children; the three youngest were by his last wife who was the daughter of Roger Skiddy, bishop of Cork and Cloyne.

Using this family connection Dean Edmund also conceived an audacious plan. Monasteries were being dissolved, their lands made over to loyal gentry. Of course Cloyne was not a monastery but a diocese; nevertheless, the policy may have put the idea into Edmund's head. He was not the only man in Ireland who was trying to appropriate Church property; lands were alienated on a grand scale in the sixteenth century. In any case, Edmund proposed to his father-in-law Bishop Skiddy that he should take a very advantageous lease on the Cloyne see lands – a fee farm grant was the most beneficial to the tenant. Bishop Skiddy is said to have agreed but the deal was never put into effect before Dean Edmund died.[16]

Now there was a hiatus for the family because Queen Elizabeth, who had come to the throne, appointed William Flynn as dean. Whether Flynn was ever able to exercise his role is unclear, but six years later Edmund's eldest son John was confirmed as dean.[17] John FitzEdmund may already have been living in the bishop's residence and he was almost certainly managing some of the Cloyne estate before he was actually appointed to his post. By now the FitzGeralds had a firm hold on Imokilly, which the new dean would exploit to its fullest extent during his long and eventful life.

---

[15] T. Clavin, 'Fitzgerald, Sir John fitz Edmund', in *Dictionary of Irish Biography* (Cambridge, 2009), pp. 880–4.

[16] Brady, *Clerical and Parochial*, vol. III, p. 3.

[17] MacCotter, 'The Geraldine Clerical Lineages of Imokilly', p. 66.

CHAPTER SIX

Sir John FitzEdmund FitzGerald

The FitzGeralds had become powerful figures in medieval Ireland and in Munster the head of the dynasty was the Earl of Desmond. The FitzGeralds in Imokilly were only a junior branch of the family and even there the senior figure was the seneschal of Imokilly, ruling from Castlemartyr. The deans of Cloyne descended from a younger son at Castle Richard. However, under the Tudors the deans rose to prominence. Their hold over the Church gave them great opportunities for enrichment but their decision to support Tudor policy proved decisive. Dean Edmund prospered and his son John FitzEdmund became a great landowner and a loyal servant of the Crown praised by Queen Elizabeth. He probably took possession of Ballymaloe in the 1570s, either buying it from his relatives or more probably through his control of Church lands. He made Ballymaloe his country seat and as he also held the bishop's castles in the town he was known as John FitzEdmund of Cloyne. Typical of the Tudor entrepreneur, he was a forceful, vigorous man who amassed a large landed fortune, survived three wars and stamped his name both on his houses and his locality.

John FitzEdmund lived in unstable times. The Tudors were determined to secure full control of Ireland and rule it as England was ruled. The Reformation was to be enforced and the great fiefdoms of the Irish nobles broken up. As the FitzGeralds rose against the Crown and Munster was convulsed, it took robust navigation of the forces in play for John FitzEdmund to survive and thrive. His cousin the seneschal at Castlemartyr owed his position to the Earl of Desmond and was loyal to his great kinsman. The deans however owed their Church appointment to the Crown and remained loyal to the monarch. Yet they too were FitzGeralds; John FitzEdmund kept a remarkable loyalty to both the seneschal and the earl throughout the terrible conflicts.

When Elizabeth came to the throne in 1558 as a Protestant claimant, crown policy on religion settled. Bishop Skiddy was obliged to retire, while new clergy were trained and introduced. The FitzGeralds were lay deans so their loyalty was more important than their theology. Dean Edmund had conformed to

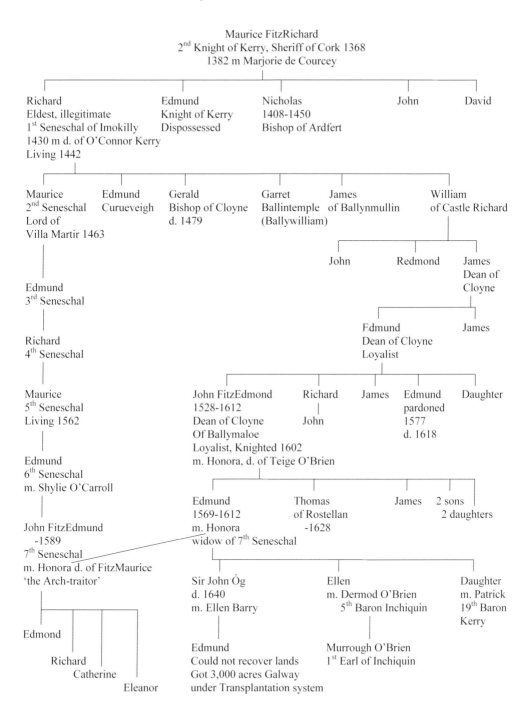

Maurice FitzRichard
2nd Knight of Kerry, Sheriff of Cork 1368
1382 m Marjorie de Courcey

Richard
Eldest, illegitimate
1st Seneschal of Imokilly
1430 m d. of O'Connor Kerry
Living 1442

Edmund
Knight of Kerry
Dispossessed

Nicholas
1408-1450
Bishop of Ardfert

John

David

Maurice
2nd Seneschal
Lord of
Villa Martir 1463

Edmund
Curueveigh

Gerald
Bishop of Cloyne
d. 1479

Garret
Ballintemple
(Ballywilliam)

James
of Ballynmullin

William
of Castle Richard

John

Redmond

James
Dean of
Cloyne

Edmund
3rd Seneschal

Richard
4th Seneschal

Edmund
Dean of Cloyne
Loyalist

James

Maurice
5th Seneschal
Living 1562

John FitzEdmond
1528-1612
Dean of Cloyne
Of Ballymaloe
Loyalist, Knighted 1602
m. Honora, d. of Teige O'Brien

Richard

John

James

Edmund
pardoned
1577
d. 1618

Daughter

Edmund
6th Seneschal
m. Shylie O'Carroll

Edmund
1569-1612
m. Honora
widow of 7th Seneschal

Thomas
of Rostellan
-1628

James

2 sons
2 daughters

John FitzEdmund
-1589
7th Seneschal
m. Honora d. of FitzMaurice
'the Arch-traitor'

Sir John Óg
d. 1640
m. Ellen Barry

Ellen
m. Dermod O'Brien
5th Baron Inchiquin

Daughter
m. Patrick
19th Baron
Kerry

Edmond

Richard

Catherine

Eleanor

Edmund
Could not recover lands
Got 3,000 acres Galway
under Transplantation system

Murrough O'Brien
1st Earl of Inchiquin

The principal sources for this pedigree are Hayman, S, *Unpublished Geraldine Documents* and Caulfield, R, *Council Book of the Corporation of Youghal*, 1878, p x-xi

FitzGerald Family Tree.

reformation policy but he died two years after Elizabeth's accession. Thady Flynn technically became the dean for four years but John FitzEdmund was actually in the post and by 1566 when his position was confirmed he had become important to the Crown as conditions in Munster worsened.[1]

When he got his father's job, John FitzEdmund was in his late thirties. He was the eldest son but illegitimate, although this did not prejudice his inheritance as he became dean, was resident in Cloyne Castle and received about 3,000 acres of land from his father.[2] As dean he managed the estates of Cloyne diocese, and because the bishop resided in Cork he had a free hand. The land was tenanted on a variety of leases but usually passed on by inheritance.

John FitzEdmund had his own property portfolio and bought more. His acquisitions in the 1560s were modest in comparison with his later ones, but significant enough. They brought in rent, and with an increased cash flow he could make further purchases.

Ballymaloe then was held by FitzGerald relatives. Since the seneschal arrived in Imokilly the family had proliferated, taken possession of some good holdings and married into local landowning families: the Whites at Mogeely were John FitzEdmund's cousins. The Ballymaloe land may have been split up: in a later schedule it appears as two holdings, one of 160 acres, the other as half a ploughland.[3]

John FitzEdmund and his cousin the seneschal inherited at about the same time and were both named John FitzEdmund. The seneschal inherited his father's fortress, the Castle of Imokilly at Castlemartyr, along with 36,000 acres. Both dean and seneschal were men of standing in Imokilly but neither of them had much time to get used to their positions before the whole area erupted in war. Both men had to make a choice. The seneschal went into rebellion; the dean followed his father's strategy of supporting the Crown.

The Earl of Desmond was detained in the Tower of London and in 1568 he wrote to both the dean and the seneschal asking the two men to aid his countess in collecting rents and keeping the peace on his lands.[4] At that stage the two John FitzEdmunds were friends and colleagues but Imokilly was already a disturbed area; government commissioners reported to Dublin that 'certain kerne' lay in ambush for them, 'but Lord Barrymore and John FitzEdmund,

---

[1] T. Clavin, 'Fitzgerald, Sir John fitz Edmund', in *Dictionary of Irish Biography* (Cambridge, 2009), p. 881.

[2] R. Caulfield, *The Council Book of the Corporation of Youghal* (Guildford, 1878), Appendix D.

[3] Ibid., Appendix C.

[4] *Calendar of State Papers, Ireland* (hereafter *CSPI*), *1509–1573*, 18 Nov. 1568.

Dean of Cloyne, met them and led them to Barry's Court', and safety.[5]

By 1569 James FitzMaurice FitzGerald was in open rebellion on religious grounds, claiming to act for the earl. All over Munster the FitzGerald leaders took up arms to resist the government's plans. The seneschal saw the Earl of Desmond as his liege lord and fought loyally for the Desmond interest throughout the terrible conflicts which followed.

The dean took the opposite course, supporting the government and raising troops among his tenants and retainers to man the castles he owned against the insurgents. In return he was made sheriff of County Cork in 1569 and was authorised to impose martial law the following spring.[6] Imokilly had become the scene of violent disorders; Sir Henry Sidney sacked Castlemartyr, smashing part of the wall, took the seneschal's stronghold and left an English garrison there. Then John Perrot was sent as lord president of Munster. In his role as sheriff John FitzEdmund was under Perrot's command. The new lord president was said to be the illegitimate son of Henry VIII and if it was true, he had his father's intelligence and ruthlessness. He hanged 800 men in Munster and forced FitzMaurice into submission.

The dean had served loyally and now pressed for reward. He sent a petition to Dublin Castle, which stated that:

> As Sheriff of Cork he has served for two years against James FitzMaurice and maintained a great number of horsemen, galloglass, shot and kern upon his own cost. He has killed many of the rebels and has not spared the execution of his own followers and nearest friends when they have forsaken him and sided with the rebels. The rebels have burnt his towns and villages, to the utter banishing of the inhabitants and robbed his goods and cattle. He has been brought from gentleman of good ability to live in extreme poverty. He is not able to maintain himself and his people about him in the service of the queen. The late lord deputy, Sir Humphrey Gilbert, Mr Jasper Horsey, Lord Deputy Fitzwilliam, the president of Munster and Mr Edward Berkeley can vouch for his service.
>
> Prays for the fee farm of the monastery of Chore, abbey of Tracton, parsonage of Ballymartyr and Corkbeg and the common gaol in Cork city, decayed, called King's Castle, which he will rebuild if he has the constableship and a fee for him and his heirs.[7]

---

5 Ibid., 23 Jan. 1568.

6 T. Clavin, 'Fitzgerald, Sir John fitz Edmund', in *Dictionary of Irish Biography* (Cambridge, 2009).

7 M. O'Dowd (ed.), *CSPI, 1571–1575* (Kew, 2000), 1572.

Unable to keep up the defence of Cloyne, John FitzEdmund withdrew to London while his petition was answered. He had made a good impression with the queen's officials; Sir Henry Sidney was sympathetic. In due course the officials decided that John FitzEdmund should be granted Chore Abbey at Ballinacurra and several parsonages. Sidney also recommended the constableship should be granted to 'this man who is meet for it'.[8] An order was received from the privy council with instructions from Lord Burghley, the queen's chief minister, and a short time later, a warrant came from Queen Elizabeth herself recording 'FitzEdmond's loss sustained in service' and referring to him as 'an old servitor'.[9] Unfortunately the warrants were not followed up, but when the lord deputy explained this to the dean, John FitzEdmund answered, 'Though her Majesty give me nothing I will be nothing the less dutiful, and yet for my dutifulness I lost a great part of that I had.' FitzWilliam advised that the dean had 'abidden much smart for his duty's sake.'[10] It would make a good example for others if he was seen to be well rewarded. In due course he received the property at Ballinacurra and the constableship.[11]

With recommendations from the highest quarters, John FitzEdmund returned to Cloyne and thought once more of the fee farm grant. A new bishop had arrived, a man named Mathew Shehan who had studied in Oxford, Cambridge and Paris. Whether Shehan was an academic who did not understand legal documents or whether he was advised by the authorities to treat the dean well, he signed up where Bishop Skiddy had delayed. Leases had to be signed by the bishop as well as the dean and chapter. John FitzEdmund had filled the chapter with his associates so in Cloyne he had a free hand: the bishop was the obstacle. This time it all went smoothly. In 1575 Bishop Shehan signed a fee farm grant for the entire Cloyne see lands for a single payment of forty marks and an annual rent of five marks. The proper rental value was probably £300 a year. In later years the agreement became a joke and the bishop of Cloyne was known as the bishop of five marks. The grant then had to be signed by the chapter. It would not look well if the dean signed a grant to himself, so to give the deal some cover, the bishop was asked to make the grant to Richard FitzMaurice, John's cousin, who then sold it on to the dean.[12]

---

8   Ibid., 2 July 1572, no. 291.
9   O'Dowd (ed.), *CSPI, 1571–1575*, 13 July 1572.
10   Ibid.
11   *The Irish Fiants of the Tudor Sovereigns during the Reigns of Henry VIII, Edward VI, Philip & Mary, and Elizabeth I* (Dublin, 1994), Elizabeth, No. 2696. John FitzEdmond is 'of Clohermony' which is in Fermoy barony and may have been his principal landholding before the grant from the queen and the fee farm grant.
12   Brady, *Clerical and Parochial,* vol. III, pp. 2–3.

The fee farm grant meant that John FitzEdmund held the head lease for the whole of the Cloyne cathedral estate. It included the demesne lands of about 500 acres and six other valuable holdings as well as the bishop's castle in Cloyne with its garden and adjoining land. On part of this land in the town the dean built a new house, for some time known as the manor house, then as the bishop's palace and now Cloyne House. He had a stone carved with his initials IGE and the date 1585, which was inserted into the wall. IG stands for Johannes Geraldus and E for Eques – soldier or horseman – to signify his leadership in the recent rebellion.[13]

Included in the Cloyne properties was Ballymaloe. Cloyne then was a busy cathedral town with a market and commercial traffic for nearby Cork harbour. A gentleman of the time with the status of John FitzEdmund needed a country house and the dean decided that Ballymaloe would suit him well. It was in a pleasant position, had excellent land and was not far from the town where his business interests were centred.

Not long after the legal papers were signed, John FitzEdmund took possession of Ballymaloe. This was not the last time that the dean dispossessed his relatives in pursuit of property. When he moved into Ballymaloe it was a late medieval tower house and bawn in the style of the previous century. John FitzEdmund must have modernised the house when he first settled himself there, but the countryside was still very unsettled and defence was a high priority. The bawn walls provided protection for the tower house and those structures were only remodelled when it was safer. The farm buildings too, although made of timber, were stout, with thick walls and heavy wooden doors. The bawn wall and the stone tower house within it were not impregnable, but with careful maintenance Ballymaloe was very hard to penetrate unless the enemy had siege weapons. At this stage the rebellious Geraldines had substantial manpower but they were at a disadvantage in weaponry, which proved a decisive factor.

John FitzEdmund now owned over 10,000 acres which he farmed in a commercial way. He made a good marriage, to Honor O'Brien, niece of the Earl of Thomond. His eldest son Edmond was born in 1569, the year of FitzMaurice's rebellion. Other children followed, so when they moved into the new manor house in Cloyne and established Ballymaloe as their country seat, the dean had a boisterous family.

---

[13] A.A. Luce, *The Life of George Berkeley* (Edinburgh, 1949), p. 173; H. Lynch, 'The Bishop's Palace', in Ó Loingsigh, *Book of Cloyne*, pp. 139–42; H.T. Fleming, 'Some of the History of the Castell and See Demesne of Cloyne', *JCHAS*, 2nd ser. vol. IX, no. 60, 1896, pp. 209–23.

But John FitzEdmund only had full legal title to Ballymaloe for four years before war broke out again with even greater ferocity. In the spring of 1573 the seneschal and FitzMaurice gave themselves up to the lord deputy and were pardoned. The Earl of Desmond was released in November and left London to return to his fiefdom of 600,000 acres and the expectations of his kinsmen. In the same month the seneschal regained Castlemartyr. Two years later, he and FitzMaurice went abroad looking for military support but the seneschal quickly returned and for some years lived uneventfully at Castlemartyr.[14] At the same time the dean was establishing a fine household at Ballymaloe; but peace was not to last.

FitzMaurice returned in July 1579 with papal troops and immediately the seneschal joined him in rebellion. A brave and skilful fighter, he played a leading role and was several times reported killed. The Earl of Desmond was proclaimed a traitor, which threw him from an uncertain position into rebellion. Government forces poured into Munster and ferocious fighting occurred in Youghal. Sir Walter Raleigh, a handsome and ambitious officer who was serving under Lord Grey, was ambushed by the seneschal at the ford in Ballinacurra. This was an important junction where the road to Cork crossed the Owenacurra River. It was also the site of the dissolved monastery of Chore which had been awarded to John FitzEdmund. Raleigh was in peril but escaped and later returned to take Castle Chore with its command of the road to Cork.

Sir Warham St Leger, the president of Munster, reported to Burghley in November 1579 that:

'All the Geraldines [are] confederates except for Sir James FitzGerald of the Decies, Sir Thomas of Desmond, and his son James, and Mr John FitzEdmund of Cloyne. All Munster bent to the Popish religion and make no reckoning of perjury. The traitors burn all the corn they may get, and demolish all castles. No doubt the traitors will have foreign aid.'[15]

The Earl of Ormond, head of the Butler family, commanded the crown forces in Munster so the rebellion continued the old Butler–FitzGerald feud. It was becoming a total war for control in Ireland, with scorched earth tactics and terrible destruction.

John FitzEdmund held firm as a government supporter throughout. His tenants were murdered by Lord Barry of Barryscourt who was now in rebellion

---

14 Clavin, 'Fitzgerald, John fitz Edmund' d. 1589 (seneschal) *Dictionary Irish Biography* (Cambridge, 2009).

15 *CSPI, 1574–1585*, 15 Nov. 1579.

and who burned his own castle to the ground to prevent Raleigh taking and garrisoning it. As a result, the local governor asked Sir Francis Walsyngham, one of Queen Elizabeth's principal secretaries, to comfort John FitzEdmund with a letter, and procure a concordatum. If Cork refused to admit all his soldiers the governor would have to 'trust to John FitzEdmund's three castles'.[16] One of these castles was Ballymaloe but John FitzEdmund also had Cloyne Castle and Ballycotton, as well as property in north Cork.

Sir Warham St Leger's opinion was that 'the Irish are not to be reclaimed by courtesy but with severe justice and rigour'. He reported that John FitzEdmund of Cloyne was 'miserably plagued by the rebels'. A figure was given for his losses: £6,157 'besides the burning of the town of Cloyne, the Castle of Ballycottyne and certain murders'. In west Waterford thirty-six towns were burned by Desmond's forces and 7,000 cattle driven off.[17]

That autumn John FitzEdmund wrote to Walsyngham himself, reminding Elizabeth's security chief that he had already suffered during the FitzMaurice rebellion and announcing that 'the Geraldines and Barrys do daily watch and devise to bereave me of my life'.[18] He was ruthless against the rebels himself; it was said he hanged his own brother James. The dean pleaded with the government for twelve horsemen and thirty or forty foot in pay to keep the six castles which he had manned himself since the beginning of the rebellion.[19]

By the spring of 1582 many of the rebel leaders had been killed but the Earl of Desmond was still at large in Kerry. Sir Warham St Leger reported plague and famine; sixty to seventy people died every day in Cork. 'The Traitors taste not of the famine and enjoy the wholesome air of the fields. John FitzEdmunds had 600 persons and now has not 30.'[20]

Sir Walter Raleigh, who was now in favour with Queen Elizabeth and became an ally of the dean, also wrote to the Earl of Leicester 'to commend unto your Honour's consideration, the pitiful estate of John Fitz-Edmonds of Cloyne, a gentleman, and the only man untouched and proved true to the Queen, both in this and the last Rebellion'.[21]

The queen responded quickly, sending an order from Greenwich to the lord

---

[16] Ibid., 4 Aug. 1580.

[17] Ibid., 24 Apr. and 18 May 1581.

[18] Ibid., 20 Apr. 1582.

[19] Ibid., Oct. 1581.

[20] Ibid., 20 Apr. 1582.

[21] Harleian Mss no. 6993, iii, quoted in T.C. Croker, *Researches in the South of Ireland* (London, 1824), section 13, p. 239.

deputy to give John FitzEdmund an annuity of 100 Irish marks and a grant of 100 marks of lands from the escheats in Munster. Wholesale confiscation was being organised and plantation planned.[22]

The queen was also changing policy. The war had been long, destructive and very expensive; she wanted it brought to a swift end. Pardons were offered to the lesser rebel gentry. Lord Barry surrendered in May but it was only after the execution of his aged mother that the seneschal also submitted on terms. He was sent to Dublin but Ormond pleaded for him to be pardoned, which was granted. He returned to Castlemartyr and married Honora, the daughter of James FitzMaurice who had been killed during the war. They had two daughters and two sons.[23] Lord Barry also returned to Barryscourt and lived to a ripe old age. For the Earl of Desmond, the end came in November 1583 when he was hunted down among the wet winter woods of Kerry and put to the sword. The Desmond power had been broken.

The queen was inclined to mercy, so John FitzEdmund helped to arrange pardons for some of his neighbours and relatives. In return he got some cheap land purchases from his clients. But many landowners had distressed estates. John FitzEdmund offered mortgages over their land which gave him possession of their property, which he did not relinquish and which helped to build up his landed fortune.[24]

Pardons had been given but much land had been confiscated, most importantly that of the Earl of Desmond himself. Crown policy was to award escheated land to 'undertakers' who would bring in new settlers and so repopulate the province with loyal Protestants. The seneschal's lands were vulnerable to confiscation; the vice-treasurer Sir Henry Wallop thought him 'the most dangerous man that is left in that province'.[25]

John FitzEdmund, however, was in a strong position to benefit from plantation. He had suffered appalling attacks and depredations, had held his men firm against the rebels, had been regularly noted in reports by all the queen's officers and was now in personal correspondence with the queen's leading ministers in London – Burghley and Walsyngham. He was also just the sort of energetic proprietor that the government hoped to see in Munster. But the dean held land

---

22   *CSPI, 1574–1585*, 16 May 1582.
23   'Fitzgerald, John Fitzedmond', in S. Leslie (ed.), *Dictionary of National Biography* (Oxford, 1921), referring to R. Dunlop's entry in the *Dictionary of National Biography* (Oxford, 1889).
24   P. MacCotter, 'The Geraldine Clerical Lineages of Imokilly', in D. Edwards, *Regions and Rulers in Ireland, 1100–1650* (Dublin, 2004), pp. 54–78.
25   *CSPI, 1586–1588*, 30 May 1586.

on various tenures; the proposed plantation might touch on his own interests, some of which were held from the Desmond estate.

A parliament was called in 1585 in which John FitzEdmund sat for County Cork. Once they were all gathered in Dublin he joined other landowners in protesting against the Munster plantation. Then a rather dangerous paper was produced – a feoffment or grant by which the Earl of Desmond had passed his estate to his son before he was ever tainted as a rebel. John FitzEdmund had been a signatory and he now testified warmly as to its legality, helping to validate the document. This was extremely awkward for the government: if the document was genuine it would nullify the Act of Attainder by which the Desmond estate was to be forfeited and all the Crown plans for the plantation would be destroyed.[26]

Sir Henry Wallop was appalled. He had come to Ireland unwillingly and found his job there extremely difficult. If the plantation did not go ahead, his position would be in jeopardy. Undertakers were already in discussion with the government and advertisements had been put out for settlers. Wallop, however, played a trump card by proving treason in the form of a pact which had been signed by the earl and which included among the signatories John FitzEdmund himself. Wallop claimed to have found it during the sack of Desmond's castle at Askeaton. Suddenly the dean's good record was exploded. Reports were sent to London and Burghley noted John FitzEdmund's part in the two documents 'to his great shame and reproof, of which I informed her Majesty who allowed of [Wallop's] good service, and condemned him of his lewdness as he well deserved'.[27]

His behaviour was completely unacceptable to the officials, but John FitzEdmund defended his signature on the earl's trust deed to his son as a 'thing of conscience and honesty before God and the world'. At the time, the earl had not been legally tainted in any way whereas the dean believed he should help and support his kinsman so long as he remained a loyal subject of Her Majesty. John FitzEdmund was supported by one of the Munster justices who considered him a gentleman, 'wise and considerate in all his doings, of great learning in good arts, and approved loyalty in all times of trial, just in his dealings, and may serve as a pattern to the most of this country'.[28]

Queen Elizabeth may have suspected that the document which Wallop claimed to have found at Askeaton might not be genuine – it had after all saved his job. Or she may have thought John FitzEdmund was too useful to alienate. She made no further trouble for him. Besides, Elizabeth wanted an end to war with its high

---

26 Ibid.

27 Ibid., 26 & 31 May 1586.

28 *CSPI, 1588–1592*, 30 Sept. 1588.

costs and losses, and she was determined to avoid further unrest. If the great men of Munster returned to loyalty and remained at peace, they could avoid dispossession. The seneschal was treated carefully, but in 1587 he was suspected of complicity with Spain and rearrested. There was considerable discussion about his future and about the extent of the plantations. The privy council decreed 'The Seneschal of Imokilly to enjoy the profit of his lands', but he died unexpectedly soon afterwards while still in Dublin Castle.[29] His eldest son was only eighteen months old at the time. The boy was confirmed as heir to Castlemartyr but could not inherit the position of seneschal. Some records suggest that title went to the dean, but the crown officers now ran Munster and the role was redundant. John FitzEdmund however played a key role in the administration of Cork, as sheriff and MP and as the leading magnate in Imokilly.[30]

So John FitzEdmund proceeded to build up his estate. From the confiscated lands in County Kerry he received 20,000 acres. It was mountainous – not good land like his fine acres at Ballymaloe – but for rough grazing it was extensive. Another 5,000 acres or more in County Limerick was his by royal grant, as were the abbeys of Kinsale, Timoleague and Castlelyons. The 10,000 acres in west and north Cork which he acquired over the next decade came by mortgage.[31] Under Irish law as it then stood the lender enjoyed the lands until the debt was paid, and many mortgages ended in a change of ownership.

To take possession of confiscated land in the west was one thing, but the dean was not afraid of seizing the estates of his neighbours and relatives in Imokilly. Here he picked up land by a mixture of methods, some legal and some fraudulent. Much was acquired by mortgage, some by offering protection from confiscation, some by legal trickery and some it seems by intimidation. In all, he had 42,000 acres in Imokilly by the end of his life. He seems to have developed a land hunger which could hardly be assuaged. A later tribunal witness testified that one Morris Oge FitzGerald 'enjoyed [his father Richard's] lands until old Sir John's time, who did thrust out Richard's children after his death'. Likewise the descendants of James, the dean's cousin, of Ballywillin and Carrigacotter, were 'thrust out by ould Sir John'.[32]

The lands he took possession of in Imokilly came from many of the leading families; he acquired 4,000 acres of Power land by mortgage, 6,500 from the

---

[29] Ibid., 21 Jan. 1589.

[30] Ibid.; Dunlop, 'Fitzgerald, John Fitzedmond' *Dictionary National Biography*, (London, 1889).

[31] Clavin, 'Fitzgerald, Sir John fitz Edmund', *Dictionary of Irish Biography*, (Cambridge, 2009).

[32] Caulfield, *Council Book Youghal*, 1878, pp. xii–xiii.

Condons of Corkbeg, 3,000 from Kennafick of Ring, as well as lands belonging to Carew, Uniack, McCotters, Magner and Hodnett.[33] He also swept up the small holdings of less-well-off relatives around Cloyne. In all, his landholdings totalled 84,000 acres. This does not compare with great palatinate holdings like that of Desmond, but the queen's aim had been to reduce those – even the undertakers were given a maximum of 40,000 and had to bring in tenants to create workable holdings. Allowing the dean to sweep up land on such a vast scale did not conform to Crown policy.

John FitzEdmund was unusual, but not unique. He was unusual because he stood out against his kinsmen and hoovered up the estates of his neighbours and relatives illegally; he was not unique because other aspiring entrepreneurs were hungrily picking up land wherever they could. Sir Walter Raleigh was undertaker in the Blackwater valley to the east of Imokilly, had the Castle of Chore at Ballinacurra and tried to get Barryscourt. He and John FitzEdmund struck up a warm friendship. A sharp young lawyer named Richard Boyle arrived in Dublin in 1588 looking for employment. By the time he arrived in Munster at the end of the century he was well on his way to a landed fortune and coming closer to Ballymaloe. The great medieval fiefdoms were ending but the Elizabethan adventurers were ascendant. It was this modernising spirt of commerce which enthused John FitzEdmund.

He was a man of his time, an improving landlord with well-stocked land, the produce of which he exported to England. Large flocks of sheep and goats suggest he was in the woollen trade. In the 1570s he had a herd of over 3,000 cattle, with 1,000 horses and 1,500 pigs.[34] He owned six watermills, and once he took possession of the Chore Abbey lands near Midleton he had fish pools. Possession and development of the settlement there by John FitzEdmund helped to create the town of Midleton. There were several castles near this important junction which he or Raleigh held – Castle Redmond was John FitzEdmund's – so they controlled the main road at the vital river crossing.[35] Among his letters to the government are requests for export permits and complaints over delays regarding his shipments of grain to Bristol. He was not just a rentier but an active man of business. He had all the characteristics of the age: a tremendous entrepreneurial energy, a reputation for learning and an innate generosity, reflecting the old Hiberno-Norman style. With a manor in Cloyne and a fine country property nearby, he could live this lifestyle to the full.

---

[33] MacCotter, 'The Geraldine Clerical Lineages of Imokilly', pp. 70–1.

[34] Clavin, 'Fitzgerald, Sir John fitz Edmund', *Dictionary of Irish Biography*, (Cambridge, 2009).

[35] *Patent Rolls of James I, 1608* (Dublin, 1987), p. 474.

Physically, the dean was a robust man who lived to old age, full of vigour and ideas. At Ballymaloe he entertained lavishly and was known for his hospitality. His wife Honor would do the honours of the house when guests arrived. His sons were brought up in lavish style but given a modern education. He had two daughters and five sons – although genealogists disagree and Honor may not have been the mother of all his children. One of his younger sons, James, was sent to study law at the Inns of Court in London, where Raleigh acted as mentor. Edmund and Thomas were both destined to inherit large estates; both married and raised families in Imokilly. Gerald later caused trouble over inheritance.

John FitzEdmund was now in a position to invest in Ballymaloe and it must have changed enormously under his ownership. He was known for his hospitality so we can assume he improved the house and made it comfortable in the style of the times. He was now a great magnate and at Ballymaloe he could enjoy his wealth and entertain lavishly. The great kitchen with its wide fireplace was the scene of hectic preparation as meats were roasted and delicious puddings prepared. The Elizabethans were explorers, gardeners and plant-hunters; new foods and better recipes came to their tables. Wine was imported to nearby Cork harbour where ships came in from Bordeaux. It was a simple matter to bring the casks out to Ballymaloe for the dean's splendid dinners.

He was a blend of the old Ireland – with its great fiefdoms where mighty magnates had troops of retainers and warriors, housed in stone castles but living in lavish style – and the Elizabethan urge to build and develop. The time was right for men of purpose with bold ideas, so John FitzEdmund fitted the moment.

In religion he was ambivalent. As a loyal servitor of the queen, he attended the new Protestant services but he allowed Catholic priests to officiate in Cloyne cathedral and maintained Franciscan friars in Timoleague where he owned property. This left him open to further attack by the English administrators.[36]

Trouble had not left him, nor had it left Ireland. A new chief justice was sent to Munster, William Saxey, who lent an ear to complaints lodged by the dean's enemies. The O'Noonans in particular, supported by one of the undertakers, Hugh Cuffe, accused John FitzEdmund of seditious speeches, both against the English and for Catholicism. Saxey was among the influx of English officials into Ireland. He disliked the country and he disliked John FitzEdmund. Saxey tried to indict the dean for high treason, reporting that:

John FitzEdmunds of Clone, a Geraldine, by her Majesty's favour has become a man of great authority in his country, not only commissioner of

---

[36] Clavin, 'Fitzgerald, Sir John fitz Edmund', *Dictionary of Irish Biography*, (Cambridge, 2009), p. 881.

the peace and quorum, but also trusted and employed in causes of state. He has £1,000 yearly revenue. For many years he has made show of religion and loyalty, and affection to the English, but of late he has been discovered to be an hypocrite and traitor.[37]

Saxey wanted the dean tried in England, which 'will be a good stop of some rebellion of the Geraldines in Mounster which is justly feared'. On Saxey's initiative John FitzEdmund was indicted for high treason in Dublin but was released; FitzEdmund had powerful friends. Saxey wanted him sent to England to be tried again, but there was no question of that happening.

Saxey was alarmed by conditions in Munster, without being sure how to identify the enemy. Hugh O'Neill, 2nd Earl of Tyrone had already begun his contest with Elizabeth in Ulster and clearly Saxey foresaw further bloodshed in Munster. He was right about that, but he was wrong about the dean. After O'Neill's victory at the Yellow Ford, Munster was once more in revolt with all the dispossessed FitzGeralds fighting for their lands while the new planters fled to save their lives. But John FitzEdmund never changed his strategy. He remained doggedly loyal to the Crown while once more his estates were devastated. In 1600 he withdrew to Dublin, much to the annoyance of the Munster authorities who complained that he gave too little support, but the dean was now in his seventies and no longer able to raise a body of fighting men; too many had already been killed.

He was not too old for land deals though and while in Dublin he managed to procure a grant for land at Conna which both Lord Barry and an English soldier had their eyes on. Carew, the president of Munster, was annoyed but John FitzEdmund's warrant came from the queen and Carew could only express his indignation mildly.[38]

By now old Lord Burghley had died, leaving his son Robert Cecil to take on his job as chief minister. When he wrote to Carew about the FitzGeralds of Munster, Robert Cecil sounded confident. He was hoping for a treaty with Spain which would keep the Spanish from interfering in Ireland. To reduce support for the rebels he was sending the young Earl of Desmond over. Since the rebellion and death of his father, the boy had been brought up in the Tower of London and was a docile young man; Cecil hoped his presence might rekindle loyalty in his kinsmen and turn them away from their more rebellious leaders. The presence of the earl might improve obedience to the crown. In 1600 Cecil told Carew:

---

[37] J.S. Brewer and W. Bullen (eds), *Calendar of Carew Manuscripts Preserved in the Archiepiscopal Library at Lambeth*, vol. III, 1589–1600, (London, 1869), p. 205, no. 266. January 1597.

[38] *CSPI, 1600–1601*, 5 June 1601.

There comes in the company of the young Earl a son of John FitzEdmunds, on whom the Queen hath bestowed a pension of 100 marks in reversion after his father. He hath made suits: the one, to have some men to keep his castles; the other, to surrender all his lands, and to take them in socage. For the first, for aught I see, he is rich enough and crafty enough … therefore in that, pretend you to have no warrant; for although I know he is wise, and hath kept a good form … he might do more than he doth. But I have used his son with kindness … because you know how dear he is to a good friend of ours (Raleigh), who is in Jersey. Besides he pretendeth to be much affected to this Desmond, and I see his son much follow him.[39]

Here for the first time, Cecil mentioned another legal plan of the dean's, to alter his title deeds into socage. Cecil had summed up John FitzEdmund, who he saw as a wily old fox although certainly a steadfast one. But he clearly liked the dean's son whom he seemed to know and of whom Raleigh was so fond.

John FitzEdmund and his son James felt warmly for the poor young earl who had been snatched away from his parents and brought up in the Tower. His arrival in Ireland would be difficult for the young man, so travelling with a friend might be helpful.

John FitzEdmund received Cecil's instructions on the matter and hurried home to receive his guest. The two young men duly sailed into Youghal where the earl was kissed rapturously by old women, much to his disgust. Nonetheless he was heir to a heroic father: the FitzGeralds were taking a new place in Irish folklore as champions of Catholic Ireland against the Crown. The Tower earl was not suitable for his role, however. Pale and bookish from long captivity, and weak from too much medicine, he was a creature of the queen. However, John FitzEdmund played his part, inviting the nervous young earl to Ballymaloe where he greeted him warmly. James, one of the younger sons of the house, had duly accompanied the young earl from London. Raleigh was now a great magnate in the area and both young men were in his circle. The family at Ballymaloe did all they could for the nervous youth while he was with them.

The young earl wrote to Cecil, '… we went to Mr. John FitzEdmund's house at Clone, where we had a great deal of cheer, after the country fashion, and shew of welcome'.[40]

This could refer to Cloyne Castle or to Ballymaloe, but the young man refers to the 'country fashion'. The dean was always known as John FitzEdmund of Cloyne because the town was his home, his business and the core of his property.

---

[39] Brewer and Bullen (eds), *Calendar of the Carew Manuscripts*, vol. III, p. 444, no. 457.
[40] *CSPI, 1600–1601*, James Earl of Desmond to Sir Robert Cecil, 21 Oct. 1600.

But like many men of the time he had a townhouse which was also his place of business, with his country seat a short distance away while he held much of the land between. So it is hard to be sure where guests dined and slept, but Ballymaloe offered more space and was away from the clamour and odours of the old cathedral town. Men of John FitzEdmund's standing often built deer parks; they had pasture and woodland where they could take guests hunting or hawking. To ride out from Ballymaloe on a fine day with hounds sniffing the pasture and hedgerows would be splendid entertainment for the dean's guests. It is more likely therefore that the young earl came to Ballymaloe than to the old Cross Castle in the town.

After the earl went on to Cork, the dean reported to Cecil that he wanted to help the youth 'as well for his father's sake, whom ever I entirely loved whiles he continued dutiful to his Sovereign, and for performing your honourable pleasure unto me directed on his behalf ... I entertained his Lordship to my poor ability, giving him all the best and soundest advices that I could invent, as well for continuing his loyalty to Her gracious Majesty, as also for directing him in his own private proceedings, and because I conceive a good opinion of him for the little time of trial I have of his Lordship, and having never seen him since he was a child.'[41]

After he left Ballymaloe, Earl James was received well elsewhere but when he went to a Protestant service, people saw him differently and began to turn away. Their loyalties strayed back to his cousin, also James, known as the Súgán Earl or Straw Earl since he had no legal title but was a more vigorous and war-like character than the Tower Earl. So Munster moved towards the next climax. Cecil had not pulled off a treaty; instead the Spanish were mobilising their troops, and a large force set sail for the port of Kinsale. In the north, O'Neill was pondering his strategy.

From Ulster, the dean received a request wrapped in a warning. 'Commendations from O'Neill unto John FitzEdmunds and his sons. O'Neill desireth you to come unto himself, and to fight for your conscience and the right. And if you do not so, be well assured by the will of God, that O'Neill and all that taketh his part will come and sojourn with you for a time. From the abbey of Ballymegalle, 23 February, 1600.'[42] The dean had survived two rebellions and was not intimidated.

Queen Elizabeth had been persuaded that to subdue Ireland she would have to spend money and she unwillingly agreed, but even so her new deputy, Mountjoy, had the smaller force when he faced O'Neill and the Spanish at Kinsale late in

---

[41] *CSPI, 1600–1601*, 23 Dec. 1600.
[42] Brewer and Bullen, *Calendar of the Carew Manuscripts*, no. 349, p. 363, 23 Feb. 1600.

1601. The dean had not shown a flicker of support for the rebels all through the FitzGerald eruptions and neither did he show any now. Defending his castles at his own cost, FitzEdmund's Imokilly showed a blank face to any of O'Neill's supporters but in Munster these were now few. Nor did the armies come down the eastern seaboard but through river valleys further west. They took up positions above Kinsale harbour and the battle began on Christmas Eve 1601, but it was the 2nd of January before the Spanish surrendered.

Mountjoy had come south through Clonmel and Glanworth but he returned by the coast road towards Waterford and 'the night that he left Cork he lodged at Cloyne, a town and manor-house sometime belonging to the bishop of that see, but now passed in fee farm to Master John FitzEdmunds, who gave cheerful and plentiful entertainment to his Lordship and all such of the nobility, captains, gentlemen, and others that attended upon him'.[43] This could mean that Mountjoy stayed at Cloyne Castle but Ballymaloe seems more likely as it was a spacious property close to the town and more suitable for the occasion. The lord deputy came with a large retinue which needed sizeable accommodation; the country mansion was more suitable for the great man's reception and it was at Ballymaloe that John FitzEdmund put up stone carvings to mark the occasion.

Carew was with Mountjoy and he knew intimately the loyalties of the big men of Cork. He could direct the governor of Ireland to the house of the man who above all others had held out for the queen in Munster and whom Mountjoy should honour with a visit. The lord deputy came over the hillside with his troop of riders and clattered into the outer courtyard at Ballymaloe to be welcomed by the most loyal of the FitzGeralds.

It must have been a great moment for the dean. After the trials and achievements of an eventful life, here was Her Majesty's lord deputy alighting at his door. His sons were in their middle years now: Edmund and Thomas had children. The house was made ready, a great meal was prepared and Ballymaloe bustled into action to entertain Mountjoy and his retinue. They spent the night in the house at Ballymaloe and in the morning broke their fast there.

Preparing to mount for the journey on to Youghal, the party came out of the house, Mountjoy the soldier strong and in command, John FitzEdmund the affable host and the established grandee of the area. At the doorway of the house Mountjoy bestowed a greater honour than his visit and, in the name of the queen, knighted her loyal servant there in the courtyard where all the household and military men could witness it. Then, springing up into his saddle, his men in attendance, Mountjoy gave his expressions of thanks, wheeled his horse's head

---

43 S. O'Grady (ed.), *Pacata Hibernia, vol. 2* (London, 1896), pp. 136–8.

and the cavalcade turned away down the drive, hooves thudding on the damp winter tracks.

Sir John! After all his work, travails and vast acquisitions, the dean was warm with exaltation. Soon the stone-carvers were busy again. In the courtyard where Mountjoy had honoured him, Sir John put up a stone carved with the letters EI and the date 1602. A much grander stone was finished later that year, carved with great skill and care to show his arms and Tudor roses. Everything had turned out splendidly. Although seventy-five, he was still fit and active, well able to enjoy his new status.

The queen however was in her last days. In March 1603 her long reign ended and James VI of Scotland was proclaimed king of England and of Ireland. Sir John was concerned that the land he held did not have very good title deeds; there was too much wrong with the way he had acquired it. He had already tried out the idea of a legal device on Cecil without success. But as his family had discovered years ago with the bishop, a new reign offers a new opportunity. So Sir John thought perhaps the same thing applied to kings and he might try to tidy up his title deeds through the good offices of the new monarch.

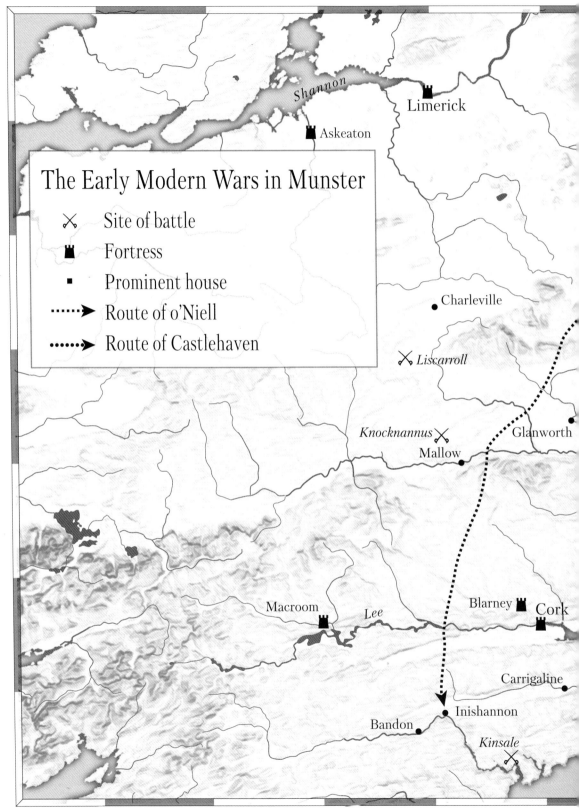

The Early Modern Wars in Munster

✗ Site of battle
🏰 Fortress
▪ Prominent house
·····▶ Route of o'Niell
●●●●●▶ Route of Castlehaven

Map 7.

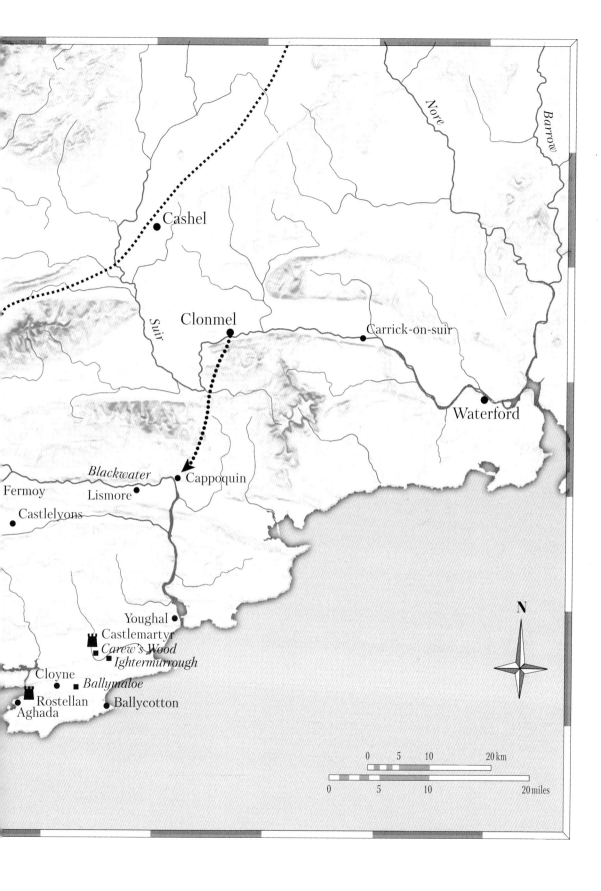

CHAPTER SEVEN

Lady Honora and Young Sir John

Sir John was now the great man of the area, with relatives and tenants in his properties – all of them dependent on him. He was resented, but he also had powerful friends. The new reign however brought changes, for Raleigh fell from favour and was imprisoned. Richard Boyle bought Raleigh's lands around Lismore and became the new great magnate of the area but even Boyle's Irish acres hardly exceeded Sir John's own. Sir John might miss his friend Sir Walter but at court he had the ear of Sir Robert Cecil who advised the new king. It soon became apparent that James I was keen to please. So Sir John set about sorting out his land titles. Surrender and re-grant was a common system for getting clean title deeds; the proprietor surrendered his property to the Crown which was then re-granted. The list of Sir John's properties is impressive. Agreed and signed in 1608, it gave FitzGerald full legal title to his long list of properties including the Cloyne castles and Ballymaloe.[1] Sir John pleaded that the queen had promised him land worth one hundred marks a year which he had not received, so King James authorised this grant to Sir John's son Edmund, 'Forasmuch as it appeareth to us, that both the said Sir John, and his said sonne, have bene always constant in their loyaltie, and readie to service …'.[2]

Now that the wars had ceased, Sir John could enjoy his fine houses and make sure that his sons would inherit the wealth he had accumulated. Sir John had married Honor O'Brien, niece of the Earl of Thomond, who brought status to the house but she was older than her husband and may not have been the mother of his children. Sir John, like his father, may have had other liaisons but the Counter-Reformation was changing Catholic attitudes and marriage seems to have become more regular after this time.

---

[1] *Patent Rolls of James I*, (Dublin, 1852), vol. 1, Pt II, 1608, no. 5, pp. 472–476.

[2] Ibid., 1607–8, no. 55, p. 496.

Sir John's eldest son Edmund married Honor of Castlemartyr, for when the last seneschal died Sir John, who was dynastic-minded, brought his widow to Ballymaloe and married her to his eldest son.[3] By the seneschal she already had four children; the eldest son Edmund was heir to Castlemartyr and was made a ward of Captain Moyle, an English soldier.[4] Honora must have brought her younger son and two daughters to Ballymaloe where they were under Sir John's protection.

Honora the daughter-in-law was the child of rebellion. She came to Ballymaloe as a widow and mother of four small children soon after her first husband died, but her father too had lived and died in rebellion. She was the daughter of James FitzMaurice, 'the Arch Traitor' of official reports who led the Earl of Desmond's troops. FitzMaurice had the barony of Kerricurrihy to the west of Cork harbour with the Castle of Carrigaline but it had been granted to an Englishman and that, coupled with the Reformation, had pushed FitzMaurice into rebellion for he was a steadfast Catholic. Honora's father and husband had both fought tenaciously, one dying in an ambush and the other in prison. So Honora came with a powerful experience of war behind her and with the same devotion to her faith as her father.

Yet she entered Ballymaloe at the invitation of Sir John the loyalist who had fought rebels with every ounce of his resources and she married his son who owned rebels' land.

Honor and Honora were the ladies of the castle. They were responsible for running it, supervising the food and drink. It was they who welcomed guests to the house and offered the best of hospitality. So these two ladies would meet visitors at the door of Ballymaloe and offer them drinks while the sisters, daughters and attendants made up the welcoming party.

Describing a visit to an Irish castle in 1620, an Englishman called Luke Gernon gives a flavour of the lifestyle:

> The lady of the house meets you wth her trayne. I have instructed you before how to accost them. Salutations paste, you shall be presented wth all the drinkes in the house, first the ordinary beere, then aquavitae, then sacke, then olde-ale, the lady tastes it, you must not refuse it.

Gernon says that guests would sit by the fire until supper time and be given sack and tobacco.

---

[3] E. Hogan, *The Description of Ireland* (Dublin, 1878), p. 179.

[4] From R. Dunlop, 'Fitzgerald, John Fitzedmund' in *Dictionary of National Biography* (Oxford, 1889), p. 132.

By this time the table is spread and plentifully furnished w[th] a variety of meates, but ill cooked and w[th]out sauce ... They feast together with great iollyty and healths around; towards the middle of supper, the harper beginns to tune and singeth Irish rymes of auncient making. If he be a good rymer, he will make one song to the present occasion.

When you come to yor chamber, do not expect canopy and curtaynes. It is very well if your bedd content you, and if the company be greate, you may happen to be bodkin in the middle. In the morning there will be brought unto you a cupp of aquavitae ... Breakfast is but the repetitions of supper. When you are disposing of yourself to depart, they call for a Dogh a dores, that is, to drink at the doore, there you are presented agayne wth all the drinkes in the house, as at yor first entrance. Smacke them over, and lett us departe.[5]

Gernon means *deoch an dorais* which means the drink of the door and was an old custom in Irish households.

This description refers to hospitality in a tower house but Sir John seems to have rebuilt Ballymaloe early in the seventeenth century. By the end of his life the castle had become a Jacobean mansion. The new house incorporated the tower house but it was extended and remodelled. Recurrent war had left the old castles battered and in need of renovation. Sir John had the wealth to rebuild and from the early seventeenth century the style of Irish country houses began to change from defensible castles to more gracious mansions. Judging by the roof timbers still in existence and by the remains of the walls, it seems clear that Sir John ended his days in an L-shaped Jacobean house. The design was probably similar to Myrtlegrove in Youghal or the much grander Ormonde Castle at Carrick-on-Suir. Houses of this period might have two floors and a gabled attic. There would be stone-mullioned windows and a central door which led to a passage which was probably panelled. The staircase was generally behind this. The house would have been in keeping with the latest ideas in design, for Sir John was now the chief magnate of the area, had been knighted by the queen's lieutenant and was extremely rich in land. The fine carved stone with Tudor roses was almost certainly over the front door, although it has been subsequently moved.

The service yard at the east end may date from this time and would have taken over the functions of the earlier bawn. The origin of the gatehouse is disputed; some experts think it dates from the same period as the tower house; others that it is later, but it was certainly remodelled. Like the turret it has arrow slits and it guards the eastern entrance beside the well. By creating this

---

[5]   L. Gernon, *A Discourse of Ireland anno 1620* (Cork, 2007), p. 360.

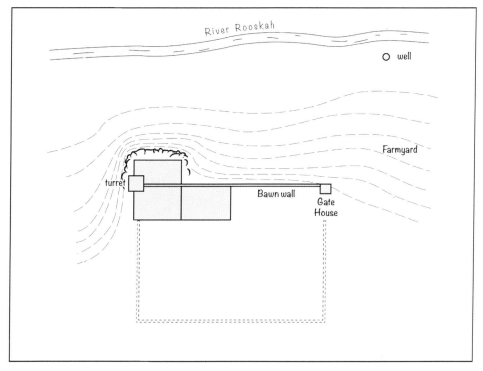

Plan 2.   Sir John FitzEdmund FitzGerald's house, late 16th – early 17th century.

yard, all domestic and agricultural activity was moved away from the front of the house.

So Ballymaloe in the early seventeenth century may have been more modern than the house described by Gernon, but the style of hospitality would hardly have altered. The ladies of the house would have brought the guests into the new reception rooms, probably on the ground floor, made sure the fire was well made up, and given them pipes and drinks until it was time for a lavish dinner with music.

Sir John's wife died before him and by the time his lands were re-granted, he was eighty-five and weakening at last, so he made his last will and testament. In it he left to 'His Majesty the King' at least some of the Church lands and tithes which he had acquired and which were listed in a schedule but which did not include the core of the Cloyne property, nor Ballymaloe.

He died early in 1612 and was buried in a splendid tomb in Cloyne cathedral. On it was carved a Latin inscription which stated, 'Here is buried a soldier of the great Geraldine family. Let his country sing his praises for ever. He was renowned for his hospitality, famous for his learning and his courage in battle was in keeping with his noble birth.' He had every reason to feel satisfied. His daughters were married, he had settled his younger son Thomas at Rostellan with a good landed estate and the enormous patrimony which would go to his eldest son Edmond had a brand new set of title deeds granted by the king.

Loss however came quickly. Only two months after his father's death the eldest son and heir was also dead. Honora became a widow for the second time. Edmond was buried with his father in Cloyne cathedral, presumably with Catholic rites. But a new dean was appointed, a Protestant like the bishop, and the Ballymaloe family no longer controlled the business of Cloyne cathedral.

Honora became the dowager lady of Ballymaloe. From her first marriage, she had four children and four more by Sir Edmond, most of whom had grown up together. By then, her eldest boy had taken possession of Castlemartyr but her Ballymaloe children were younger. Old Sir John had dominated the house but now there was a lady at its head, with children not yet of age.[6]

Because her first husband's estate had been contested, Lady Honora's claims to dower or widow's rights were not straightforward. She also had to manage her son's estate. Since he was underage when his father died, he like his step-brother was subject to the custom of wardship where other gentlemen might control both the boy and his estate. Richard Boyle was helpful to Honora; he bought land from her which raised enough money so that she could buy her son's wardship and so keep control of his lands and education. As her son at Cloyne grew up, John Óg – John the younger – and his mother had to do more business with Boyle, but it seems to have gone smoothly. Iron bars were paid by the FitzGeralds to Boyle as part of a business agreement, John Óg received a horse and in another

---

[6] The ownership of Castlemartyr has not been settled by historians. In *Burke's Guide to Country Houses*, Mark Bence-Jones records Castlemartyr as belonging to Raleigh, by which it came to the 1st Earl of Cork, a line of ownership which several other historians support. However, Castelmartyr was clearly owned by the last seneschal's son in 1641 which has been accounted for by Lord Cork returning it to the FitzGeralds, possibly in exchange for other lands. The evidence does not support this. It is not recorded among the grant to Raleigh either in the Fiants of Elizabeth or in an inventory of Raleigh's lands in the National Library of Ireland (NLI), Lismore Papers, Ms. 43,584/1. The Lismore Papers are extensive and beyond the scope of this book, but the catalogue for them only refers to Castlemartyr in connection with the Earls of Shannon a century later. In the *Calendar of State Papers Ireland* there is a discussion about the seneschal and the confiscations which is not definitive. In *The Dictionary of Irish Biography* (2009), Terry Clavin recounts that Ormond secured a pardon for the seneschal and the state papers confirm that he was to receive the income from his lands which was the position at the time of his death. The assumption of this book is that although the seneschal's great estate may have been dismembered, the fortress of Castelmartyr with its immediate lands remained in the possession of Edmund, son of the last seneschal and Honora.

deal Lady Honora gifted Boyle a goshawk in a business gesture which was then fashionable.

Honora had business loans and was seldom recorded repaying them, a situation which came to the attention of the privy council in due course.[7]

Richard Boyle became 1st Earl of Cork in 1616 and made good marriages for all his children among the aristocracy. He also took an interest in the marriage of Lady Honora's daughter, as did the lord president of Munster, for the alliances of the FitzGeralds were significant. Lady Honora wrote to Lord Cork at some length about her daughter Honora's dowry when a marriage was arranged with Patrick, 19th Baron of Kerry. Lady Honora explained the lands and sums offered in a letter to Lord Cork, 'which I and all the rest of our friends do think in conscience and in law, to be as good paiement as may be, and so I do request your honor if there should bee anie difficultie in this my demands that your lordshippe will be a mediator …'.[8]

Honora practised her Catholic religion openly and attracted attention from the authorities for it. She had property of her own in her marriage jointure, some of which she used to support the clergy. Carew complained constantly of how the gentry banded together to prevent Protestants getting local promotion and in particular he mentioned that 'My Lady Onora FitzGerald is never without some of the fathers of Rome and priests, and she gives the Romish church a yearly stipend for the livings she holds and enjoys.'[9]

A tangible memento of Honora is still in Cork. The Dominican friary in Youghal had been dissolved by the authorities in the sixteenth century but the friars hung on there with support from local gentry. They owned a relic which was venerated, a small ivory carving of the Madonna brought to Youghal centuries before from the continent. Honora gave the Dominicans a silver-gilt shrine in which to keep it, a small box with opening doors inscribed with her name and the date 1617. It is now in the Dominican friary in Cork.[10]

Young John enjoyed the enormous landed estate of his grandfather but the authorities were annoyed at how old Sir John had got the Cloyne lands and Chichester the lord deputy made an attempt to get them back. He drafted a bill 'to resume and make void' Sir John's fee farm grant of the Cloyne lands, his point being that Bishop Skiddy had only agreed to rent out small parcels but

[7] These details were given by Dr Clodagh Tait of UCC at the Youghal Celebrates History conference 2015.

[8] NLI, Ms. 43, 266/6.

[9] Brewer and Bullen (eds), *Calendar of the Carew Manuscripts*, vol. V, p. 198.

[10] S. Hayman, 'The Ecclesiastical Antiquities of Youghal', *Proceedings and Transactions of the Kilkenny and South-East of Ireland Archaeological Society*, vol. 3, no. 2, 1855, pp. 326–36.

'by manifest fraud' the whole estate had been included in the document, which Bishop Shehan had not checked properly. Chichester's bill would make the grant void but the heir should be compensated for 'the erection of any new building which is now standing on the premises' which meant the new manor house at the east of the town.[11]

The heir was John, named for his grandfather but not yet of age. Honora could hardly protect her son's estate by herself but luckily she had the help and support of her brother-in-law Thomas at Rostellan who was John's guardian.[12] The family talked things over and decided to hide old Sir John's will. If it was known that he had given some Church lands back, their legal case would weaken. Better to stand firm on the re-grant and fight their case. Before anything was done, Chichester became ill and retired; the issue of the Cloyne lands was not followed up – for now.

Young John inherited and was voted a knight of the shire by his fellow gentry. He must have been confident about his property because in 1624 he petitioned to build a pier in Ballycotton – on Church property – from which he would collect the customs duties.[13]

Young Sir John – Sir John Óg – was an adult by then and married to Ellen Barry, daughter of David, Viscount Buttevant. They had probably not been married long when they had a harp made for them, a cast of which is on display at Ballymaloe today. The harp was a highly ornamented instrument, carved with foliage and animals and two coats of arms. Inscriptions were also carved onto it which tell us – 'Donagh, son of Teige made me' and 'John FitzEdmund and Ellen Barry caused me to be made'. 'I am the queen of harps', the carving announced.

On to the sections of the instrument the maker carved the names of the principal members of the household, the steward and chamberlain, the cook and the butlers for wine and beer. The resident harpist was Gilla Patrick MacCridan and his assistant Dermot MacCridan – 'two accomplished men, whom I had to care me'. The date carved onto the harp is 1621.[14]

How clearly that instrument evokes the household at Ballymaloe with its Gaelic-Norman culture. Irish was still spoken and the familiar music played. A team of professionals ran the large household. In the evenings the rippling melodies of the harp filled the dining hall as red meat was eaten, wine was poured

---

[11] *CSPI, James I, 1611–1614*, no. 702, pp. 367–8.

[12] D. Ó Murchadha, *Family Names of County Cork* (Dublin, 1985), p. 147.

[13] Brady, *Clerical and Parochial*, vol. III, p. 4.

[14] The harp is described in W. Fitzgerald, 'Descriptions of Two Fitzgerald Harps of the Seventeenth Century', *Journal of the County Kildare Archaeological Society*, vol. VIII, 1915–17, pp. 133–49. See Appendix 2, p. 142.

and voices spoke in both English and Irish. The Earl of Cork had a harper at Lismore but the earl was English and a Protestant. Ballymaloe was a great house of the Munster FitzGeralds. Even if the earldom of Desmond had fallen, the traditions lived on.

John and Ellen had seven children, five sons and two daughters, who grew up in the early years of Charles I's reign.[15] The children had cousins at Castlemartyr for Edmund was now a married man with two sons. John Óg's sister Ellen had moved to Clare when she married; her husband was Dermod O'Brien, Baron Inchiquin, and her eldest boy was Murrough O'Brien, born in 1614. This son would grow up to become a military commander with an infamous name. But for now, Ireland was at peace. Lady Honora died in 1628 leaving her son and daughter-in-law installed at Ballymaloe with their children and household. There were relatives all around, most of them settled in properties which Sir John Óg owned or for which he held the head lease.

Men in politics who visited Dublin talked of the exclusion of Catholics from parliament and Cloyne cathedral now had a Protestant dean, but the FitzGeralds used the little church at Ballyoughtera at Castlemartyr and could maintain their Catholic services. Trouble started in earnest for Sir John Óg when King Charles sent his vigorous lord deputy Thomas Wentworth to Dublin. Wentworth had express instructions to get back all the Church of Ireland's property which had been so shamelessly pilfered and alienated during the last two reigns. In fact Archbishop Laud wrote to Wentworth, 'I hope you will join Sir Thomas [sic] FitzEdmonds to the rest of his Fellows, and make him vomit up Cloyne.'[16] This time the Crown meant business. Wentworth was tough and efficient; even Boyle could not withstand the new courts he set up. Sir John Óg saw clearly enough that he would have to settle. But this was serious; his principal homes – his country mansion Ballymaloe and the manor of Cloyne which his grandfather had built – would both potentially be forfeit. So would the top-quality land between Ballymaloe and Cloyne as well as the fishery at Ballycotton and other important property. It could be a catastrophe. Bishop Bramhall was to make the case for the Church, so Sir John Óg engaged his brother-in-law Patrick Lord Kerry, married to his sister Honora, to put his counter-argument.

Cloyne was to be made a separate see again; in fact a bishop had already been appointed, an Englishman named George Synge, so there would be a resident bishop in Cloyne where the FitzGeralds had had a free hand for generations. Also, the new bishop would need a house.

---

15 Funeral Entries, Ulster King of Arms, (Genealogical Office) vol. 9, p. 232.

16 W. Knowler (ed.), *The Earl of Strafford's Letters and Dispatches*, vol. 1 (London, 1739), p. 255.

Sir John and Lord Kerry had to settle; there was no chance of holding on to all the Cloyne lands; even Lord Cork had had to settle, despite his position in government and skills in business. Afterwards Sir John Óg criticised his brother-in-law, for he did in effect lose his hold on Ballymaloe and the Cloyne estate.[17] Instead, the bishop was awarded the Cloyne manor with 600 acres and the Ballycotton fishery while Sir John Óg received a sixty-year lease on the remainder at an increased rent. Wentworth signed the agreement in 1639 between hurrying to England to fight the rebellious Scots, for trouble was brewing again.[18]

Losing the plum properties at the heart of his estate was a bitter blow to Sir John, but in any case he fell ill of the palsy the following year and began to examine his conscience. He was plagued with guilt. The great estate bequeathed to him had been acquired by trickery and greed. Many of his relations had lost property or been reduced to tenants and Sir John knew they spoke against him. Also, he had concealed his grandfather's will. All these things weighed heavily on him so he went over to Ballyhonock to visit his cousin James FitzGerald who was then in his fifties, a little older than John, who acted as his agent and 'kept his evidences' – his deeds and records.[19]

At Ballyhonock Sir John made his will, repeating the bequest to King Charles of part of the Cloyne estate (which he now held on lease but which had been in his grandfather's will) and returning to many of his neighbours and relatives lands taken from them by his grandfather. The list was long. He also provided for his widow and children, leaving the rest to his eldest son Edmond.

James the agent at Ballyhonock called in two of his relatives as witnesses and the will was duly signed. James was to keep the will safe until Sir John's death when it was to be published. Two months later James the agent was called over to Ballymaloe where he found Sir John clearly very ill. He suffered from palsy, which had returned; he thought he would soon be unable to speak and he wanted to review his will. James read it to him and Sir John added a codicil with more bequests. He was very upset and remorseful about concealing his grandfather's will and detaining Church lands, in fact part of the will read like a confession and prayer.

This was put in the codicil: 'Jesus give me grace to order my life and the work of my body and soul'. Sir John ended, 'Grant me, Lord, by the merits of this passion and virtue of thy most excellent and glorious divinity, whatsoever thy

---

[17] Brady, *Clerical and Parochial,* vol. III, p. 6.

[18] Ibid.

[19] R. Caulfield (exhibited): Collection of several hundred original documents relating to the city and county of Cork, including the will of Sir John fitz Edmond Gerald, of Ballymaloe, *Journal of the Royal Society of Antiquaries of Ireland*, vol. V, 1880, p. 271.

wisdom knoweth most expedient to mee, which my miserable life is not worthy
to obteyne of thee at the hour of my death, when I shall be accused before that
death that thou sufferest for sinners, have mercy on my soul.'

Sir John was only forty-five but the palsy was weakening him, and he could
not grasp the pen. Attendants warmed a bullet which was put into his hand and
after a while he was able to sign his name.

He died early in January the next year.[20] His heir was his son Edmund whose
own agent was Thomas Skiddy. Skiddy duly registered the death with the Ulster
King of Arms. However, James, who had been pressed so strongly by Sir John to
publish the will, did not do so. The FitzGerald of Cloyne estate had impoverished
some but enriched others and James the outgoing agent saw how much trouble
the will might cause. He kept it locked with his private papers at Ballyhonock
while the family consulted – which is how things stood in October that year
when rebellion broke out in Ulster.

Hearing stories of atrocities, Protestants fled Ireland and Bishop George Synge
hurried away to Dublin. Edmund FitzGerald, still resident at Ballymaloe, had
little difficulty in retaking possession of the Cloyne manor along with the 600
splendid acres. All the bishop's cattle were seized along with much of his personal
property. With the country in uproar there was no-one to prevent this, especially
since Edmund had a large household staff and many men working on his land or
living in his properties, all of whom he could call upon.

However, the emerging Confederacy was not a small matter of short duration
but part of a collapse of government in London and throughout the two islands
which would alter life at Ballymaloe beyond all recognition.

---

[20] *Journal of the Kildare Archaeological Society*, vol. VIII, 1915, pp. 142–3.

CHAPTER EIGHT

The War of Three Kingdoms

When rebellion broke out violently in October 1641 it quickly led to the creation of the Catholic Confederacy based at Kilkenny which controlled most of Ireland for the rest of the decade. The government retained the east coast ports, but as their officials and troops were Protestant, the war immediately became sectarian. However, there were at least five parties active in the war, allegiances changed as circumstances altered and it was only in 1649 that almost all united behind the king's cause to resist the Puritans. By then it was too late to defeat Cromwell's forces.

In Imokilly the war was fought most intensively in 1645 but from the outbreak there were violent attacks, while unpaid troops rounded up cattle and took corn. Fortresses played a key role in the war, so it is not surprising to find many references to 'Ballymartyr' or Castlemartyr which was a mighty stronghold on the main road. It is disappointing to find few direct references to Ballymaloe but it was smaller and less strategic. It had retainers but the curtain wall had probably been altered when old Sir John built his mansion: it was not a garrison as Castlemartyr was. As a result it suffered in the rain shadow of the more military castle, but was less badly damaged. All the same, for the FitzGeralds it was a decade of fear and loss.

All the tales are of war, so reconstructing the life of the household from 1641 until the Cromwellian invasion of 1649 is not easy. The important relationship is that between two Edmund FitzGeralds: one at Castlemartyr who was the son of the last seneschal and the other at Ballymaloe who was the son of Sir John Óg – Sir John the younger. Edmund of Ballymaloe was a generation younger than his cousin at Castlemartyr and had only lost his father the previous year. He was hardly of age when the rebellion broke out and when he appears in the records it is always in connection with his cousin whose lead he clearly followed. Many commentators confuse the two families, but when legal matters or treaties are concluded the names stand together: Edmund FitzGerald of Ballymartyr and Edmund FitzGerald of Ballymaloe. Working from this we can reconstruct something of those troubled times.

A man called Henry Rugge can set the scene for us. He was a Protestant living in Youghal who wrote to John Smyth in August 1642 to give his colleague in England 'true intelligence of those occurrences which have happened in these parts since the beginning of the late universal insurrection of the Irish papists of this kingdom'. He explained where Munster was and told Smith that:

> ... this part remained 2 months quiet after all the rest had revolted, and we conceived good hopes of its continuance till about 12 days before Christmas, when certain rebels out of Leinster came in and disturbed our hoped security. The Lord President was not idle all the while, but having secured Cork (the most remarkable place of this Province) the best he could, in the extreme want of men, money [and] ammunition, with 3 troops of horse and 50 musketeers he fell upon that enemy and within a few days destroyed about 600 of the rebels.[1]

Richard Boyle, 1st Earl of Cork, was shocked to the marrow by the rebellion. He thought Ireland was stable and developing. He personally galvanised his men to hold Youghal while he sent his sons out to fight. In January 1642 he wrote to Lord Goring in England:

> All the English about us are fled, save such as have drawn themselves into castles, but are few in effect, and they are fearful. All the natives that are papists (the rest being few or none) are in open action and rebellion; except the Earl of Barrimore, who behaves himself most loyally and valiantly. But, alas! what is he with his forces amongst so many, when the whole kingdom is out? I am by commandment of the Lord President drawn hither to Yoghall to secure the same; which is the only town, that the English have to retreat unto ...

He ends: 'We are now at the last gasp; and therefore if the state of England do not speedily supply us, we are all buried alive.'[2]

The lord president of Munster, Sir William St Leger, relied on his son-in-law Murrough O'Brien, Baron and later 1st Earl of Inchiquin. This young nobleman came from a distinguished line: his father descended from Brian Boru and his mother was Ellen FitzGerald of Ballymaloe, so he was Edmund FitzGerald's

---

[1] Henry Rugge to John Smith, 'true intelligence ...'. Among the papers of Reginald Cholmondeley collected for the history of Chester and other purposes. *Fifth Report Historical MSS Commission* (London, 1876), p. 346.

[2] Quoted in S. Hayman, *Annals of Youghal* (Youghal, 1848), p. 31.

cousin. However, after his father's death, Inchiquin had been brought up as a Protestant and had married St Leger's daughter. His career depended on his Protestant credentials and he certainly identified with the Munster Protestants – defending their interests was his main war aim. His extended family however were Catholic and during the war he was often suspected of disloyalty by both sides. His extreme measures may have been attempts to prove to the Protestants that he was no papist sympathiser; his experience of war in Europe had likely taught him merciless forms of warfare. The Catholics soon had reason to fear and then hate him. Inchiquin emerged as a daring, ruthless and successful cavalry commander.[3]

Inchiquin's rival in Munster was Lord Cork's third son Roger, Viscount Broghill, who had been left to defend Lismore Castle while his now elderly father took charge in Youghal. Broghill wrote to the earl that if Lismore 'be lost, it shall be with the life of him, that begs your lordship's blessing, Your lordship's most dutiful son and servant, Broghill'.

Inchiquin lacked manpower but was confident because the Irish Confederates had no artillery. He held Cork, but the countryside was roused. Both sides lacked supplies so to feed his troops and supply Cork, Inchiquin 'was obliged to take all the cattle left in the baronies of Imokilly and Barrymore … which left the country in a deplorable condition'.[4]

We know what was happening at Ballymaloe meanwhile because in April that year St Leger sent 'true and happy news' to the lord lieutenant, naming those who were loyal to the Crown, which included Edmund FitzGerald of Ballymartyr, 'by whose care and countenance that barony of Imokilly is kept in due subjection, and the passage betwixt this city and Youghall thereby open'.[5]

The Confederate forces invariably entered Munster down the river valleys through Tipperary, which is why so much fighting was in north Cork. When a truce was called in 1643, Imokilly had been pillaged but the castles there were intact. It was the change of allegiance of Inchiquin in 1644 which brought the war thundering into east Cork. St Leger died and Inchiquin needed the presidency to hold Munster but the king gave it to another and in any case, the royalists were fighting parliament in England and could not send supplies. Parliament had better resources than the king. For Inchiquin and Broghill, the enemy was the Confederates: to both of them king and parliament were part of the legitimate government. The two men competed with each

---

[3]   J.A. Murphy, 'Inchiquin's Changes of Religion', *JCHAS*, vol. LXXII, 1967, pp. 58–68.

[4]   C. Smith, *The Antient and Present State of the County and City of Cork*, vol. II (Dublin, 1774), p. 145.

[5]   W. St Leger, '*True and happy news …*', April 1642.

other but when Inchiquin changed his allegiance to parliament, Broghill soon followed suit. Parliament awarded Inchiquin the presidency of Munster and sent supplies.

Inchiquin's position was complicated by his ancestry. After he expelled the Irish from Cork in 1644 he was clearly no friend of the Gaelic population, but it was the slaughter and burning which he inflicted on Cashel which earned him the sobriquet Murchadh na Tóiteán – Murrough the Burner – by which the notorious commander was remembered. He lived with an intense conflict of identity which the war tested to its limit. Of all the descendants of Ballymaloe, Inchiquin's life was the most dramatic and conflicted, but as a soldier he was exceptional.

The FitzGeralds had begun the war as supporters of the royal government, but when Inchiquin changed allegiance, they changed in the opposite direction. Firstly, as Catholics their natural allegiance was to Kilkenny. Secondly, the country people around them sympathised with the Confederacy which most of their kinsmen had joined. Lastly, Inchiquin was now fighting for the London parliament which was dominated by Puritans, the group which Catholic Ireland dreaded.

FitzGerald of Imokilly wrote to the Committee of the Confederates in 1644 to warn them of 'the landing of fourteen hundred of the Parliament forces, and that four of ther shipps are come up to Corcke'.[6]

Early in 1645 the Earl of Castlehaven invaded Munster with a Confederate force of 5,000 men. The war in both Britain and Ireland was fought over garrisons and defended houses, with occasional pitched battles. Castlehaven took the strongholds north of the Blackwater River but Inchiquin determined he should not possess those of east Cork. Through his mother Inchiquin was related to the owners of Ballymaloe, Rostellan and Castlemartyr but this did not stop him attacking the two latter castles to prevent Castlehaven taking and garrisoning them.

According to Castlehaven, Inchiquin took Rostellan by chasing out his relative Mrs FitzGerald and hanging two priests who were in the castle. However, Inchiquin sent a message to the priests and friars at Castlemartyr offering them an escape before he attacked but he was warned that parliament would abandon him for such behaviour.

Castlehaven had been ordered into Imokilly because 'the enemy in this province had always been victorious, beating the confederates in every encounter … so that every gentleman's house or castle was garrisoned, and kept the country

---

[6] Carte Papers, Vol. XII, p. 213, in T. Gilbert and R. Bellings, *History of the Confederation and War in Ireland, vol. III, 1646–1648* (Dublin, 1882–1891), p. 268.

in awe'. The Confederate commander used harsh methods but when Dean Boyle pleaded with him, Castlehaven retorted, 'I had orders to take all I could, and such as I thought not fit to garrison, to destroy.'[7] These were hard times in Imokilly.

Between Inchiquin and Castlehaven, the barony was devastated. Inchiquin attacked Castlemartyr and breached the walls until Edmund FitzGerald's son surrendered; then he set fire to the castle and the town. Castlehaven says that 'when I came in sight of the place, I found it taken, burning and the enemy retreating, some to Cork, others to Youghal ...'[8] He camped by Ballymartyr for two or three days and burned Cloyne and Aghada, before going on to besiege Youghal and then 'trifled out the remainder of the campaign, in destroying the harvest'.[9]

When Castlehaven moved away to the Confederate port of Waterford, he took 8,000 cows with him 'and people that I have brought out of Immikilly and this morning I shall pass them over the Blackwater ... and so the county of Waterford to be always under shelter of the army'. The FitzGerald men were Confederate officers for the rest of the war, the women and children of the household may have left for Waterford. Perhaps some of the household remained to hold Ballymaloe but the armies had despoiled Imokilly of food and the houses were no longer defensible.

There can have been few people at Ballymaloe or even Cloyne for some time since buildings were broken, cattle stolen and crops destroyed. Castlehaven had mastery over Munster but a partial truce was agreed the following year and in 1647 Inchiquin won a massive victory at the battle of Knocknannus, which gave him control of southern Ireland. This left the prospects for the FitzGeralds very poor but the war in England had changed dynamic and Irish leaders rethought their position. The Puritans had control in Britain, which gradually united all the warring parties in Ireland in support of the king. Towards the end of the war the two Edmund FitzGeralds appear in Confederate records as officers of the king and so later they could make claims for their estates.

However, it was too late for the Confederacy. Charles I was executed and the new Commonwealth government sent Cromwell to subjugate Ireland. The general met Broghill in London where he threatened to imprison him should Broghill try to join the exiled Charles II. For his campaign, Cromwell needed Broghill, who had great influence with the Irish Protestants. Broghill agreed to work for the Puritans and came back to Ireland in 1650 where he became a

---

7   Earl of Castlehaven, *Earl of Castlehaven's Memoirs* (Waterford, 1753), pp. 62–4.

8   Ibid., p. 68.

9   Ibid., p. 72; Gilbert and Bellings, *History of the Confederation and War in Ireland, vol. IV*, p. 281.

vigorous cavalry leader in the Cromwellian army. This would eventually win him the FitzGerald properties in Imokilly. Cromwell told the Council of State, 'The Lord Broghill is now in Munster; where he, I hope, will do very good offices: all his suit is for two hundred pounds to bring his wife over: such a sum would not be cast away. He hath a great interest in the men that come from Inchiquin.' Cromwell was right – the Protestants who fought under Inchiquin deserted him and the ports capitulated to Cromwell.

During the winter of 1649–50 Cromwell lodged for a time in Youghal and this may be when he came to Ballymaloe, which is still spoken of in the Boyle family. The army marched out several times with Cromwell at its head and beside him his son-in-law Ireton, who became lord deputy of Ireland. It may be on one such excursion that they came to the house, probably with Broghill, who already knew it. The courtyard walls must have been damaged but the house may have been largely intact, even if neglected and pitiful. The farm buildings then were wooden so they were unlikely to have survived intact after the pillaging of two armies.

This may be the occasion when Cromwell told Broghill of his motives for the king's execution. The New Model Army had vied for power with the Scots, hoping to make an agreement with the king, and so become dominant. When the army intercepted the king's letter detailing his negotiations with the Scots, they instead resolved on his ruin.[10]

Broghill said that he heard this story with horror, since in his heart he was a royalist – but he certainly made himself useful to whoever was in power. He was a capable man, both as a politician and as a soldier: leaders of both the Puritans and the royalists courted his support. For Broghill, working for Cromwell paid off but among his peer group he was not well-liked.

Bagwell the historian believed that Broghill and Inchiquin aimed to divide east Cork between them from the beginning. In 1650 Inchiquin was being pushed back, retreating west with the royalist army while Broghill was an officer in the advancing army of conquest. He was soon rewarded: Cromwell gave him custody of Blarney Castle, taken from the MacCarthys, but Broghill was still in arms and fought with Ireton at Limerick. He defeated Inchiquin's army near Mallow, after which his old adversary left Ireland for exile in France. Many Royalists sailed to Europe; Edmund FitzGerald of Castlemartyr died in Brussels in 1654.

The Cromwellian army retired to quarters. Cork was in their control and Colonel Phaire the regicide became governor of Cork while his officers began to reorganise the county. With the advice of Lord Broghill, the policy of

---

[10] K.M. Lynch, *Roger Boyle, First Earl of Orrery* (Knoxville, TN, 1965), p. 75; Hayman, *Annals of Youghal*, p. 45; From NLI, Ms. 473, Morrice Ms., ff. 30–3.

transplantation was formulated and the confiscations were organised. County Cork was kept for the government and the estates there were not at first given to settlers. Instead the properties were let on short leases of a few years. Ballymaloe was to become the home of several soldiers in the militarised Ireland of the late seventeenth century.

The first soldier was Colonel Peter Wallis, who apparently leased Ballymaloe from the Commissioners for Ireland in 1650. The ruined Castlemartyr was let to Colonel Robert Saunders on a seven-year lease around the same time. Unlike Phaire and Saunders, Wallis had been born in Ireland after his father bought lands in Curryglass in 1595. He was leading a troop in 1650 and he fought with Broghill at Macroom against Lord Muskerry. Wallis was part of the Cork garrison during the Cromwellian years and was recorded several times organising for disbanded Confederates to be sent overseas or arranging the drawing of lots by which the soldiers got their lands. Wallis took testimony about Inchiquin from his former troops and he enforced the articles of war.[11]

The Cromwellian army was infused with the religious experiments which raged in the 1650s. Much of the army became Baptist but Wallis, like Phaire, attended Quaker meetings.[12] The Quakers were a young but growing sect with radical ideas. The soldiers' politics were tested too as the Cromwellian regime struggled with the constitution. In 1654 both Phaire and Saunders took the side of the parliament against Cromwell's army, but Wallis remained loyal to Cromwell and his regime throughout. The following year one of the army's commanders in Ireland, Edmund Ludlow, published pamphlets criticising Cromwell's elevation to lord protector. Colonel Wallis was sent to question Ludlow, who lost his commission.[13] The following year Peter Wallis again supported the Cromwellian regime when he was a commissioner in a trial for treason regarding the security of 'His Highness the Lord Protector'.[14] Wallis was Cromwell's man.

While Wallis was residing at Ballymaloe and enforcing the Cromwellian regime, members of the Confederacy were losing their lands in a wholesale confiscation. Those who could show some loyalty to the parliament were eligible

---

[11] R. Dunlop, *Ireland under the Commonwealth*, vol. I (Manchester, 1913), pp. 25, 391, 473–4, 476.

[12] C.B. Gibson, *The History of the County and City of Cork*, vol. 2 (London, 1861), p. 120, quoting Henry Cromwell's letter to Thurloe.

[13] Smith, *Antient and Present... Cork*, vol. II, p. 175; C.H. Firth (ed.), *The Memoirs of Edmund Ludlow*, vol. I (Oxford, 1894), p. 407.

[14] C.H. Firth and R.S. Rait (eds), *Acts and Ordinances of the Interregnum*, vol. II (London, 1911), p. 1,041.

for poorer land west of the Shannon and this is what happened to Edmund FitzGerald of Ballymaloe. In 1656 he was among the transplanted Irish and was awarded 1,500 acres of confiscated land in Connaught.[15]

FitzGerald's property in Imokilly was confiscated by the Cromwellian government and used to pay its debts or to reward its soldiers. Broghill was out of Ireland in 1655 leading the government in Scotland and rising in the lord protector's esteem. He was rewarded with land: Blarney Castle was settled on him permanently by Act of Parliament. The bill went through the Commons on 5 June 1657 with a clause confirming Blarney and a second clause which awarded to Broghill 'the Castle and House of Ballymalo, Parcel of the late Possessions of Edmond Fitzgerald of Ballymalo', along with 2,000 acres contiguous to it as Lord Broghill should think convenient, with all the 'houses, messuages and appurtenances' on that land.[16]

Colonel Saunders, who had spent considerable funds at Castlemartyr and saw that Broghill might encroach on the land he held, immediately petitioned the lord protector and council to renew his lease for a longer term. He asked for fifty-one years, the lord deputy was consulted and recommended that Saunders be given a thirty-one-year lease from May 1657. Colonel Wallis was awarded land at Shanagarry.

So Ballymaloe became the possession of Roger Boyle, Viscount Broghill. By 1657 he had amassed enormous debts so he sold Blarney almost immediately. Ballymaloe became his home, and his land in Imokilly his main income. Gradually he got back the land he had inherited from his father and brought it into production, which increased his income.[17]

Broghill was a clever man, energetic like his father, charming and good at self-promotion. He was not an entrepreneur like old Lord Cork, but a military man, an able administrator and a successful politician. He was adept at knowing when tides were turning in national affairs and moving with that tide. When Cromwell died in 1658, Colonel Wallis was in confusion but for Broghill the lord protector's death did not bring confusion but a new opportunity. He was the most significant of the Munster Protestants and he led them skilfully. As a group, they were constantly insecure, lobbying or fighting to hold onto their possessions in Ireland. Each change of government brought new threats but could be used to advantage. In the unravelling after Cromwell died, Broghill used the good offices of his brother, the 2nd Earl of Cork, who had remained close to the

---

[15] Historical Manuscripts Commission, *Ormonde Mss*, vol. 2, (London, 1895–1899), p. 141.

[16] *Commons Journal*, vol. 7 (London, 1802), 5 June 1657.

[17] P. Little, *Lord Broghill and the Cromwellian Union with Ireland and Scotland* (Woodbridge, 2004), pp. 217–18.

royalists in England and who now hastened to the exiled court of Charles II to attach himself to the young king. The Boyles made an accommodation with the royal regime and were the king's loyal supporters by the time the Restoration was achieved.

In 1660 Charles II rode into London to reclaim his father's throne. The Irish Catholics who had fought for his father hoped that they too would be restored. Edmund FitzGerald of Ballymaloe had ended the war as a royalist officer and had every such hope of returning to Ballymaloe Castle and reclaiming his patrimony in east Cork.

CHAPTER NINE

A Boyle House

In the uncertain times when Cromwellian rule was collapsing, Lord Broghill left England in order to lie low at Ballymaloe. He told Whitelocke that he 'now talks with no other but his Thoughts, his small library and yet ... would not change that life, for a kings, or what is more a Generalls'.[1] His east Cork neighbours were soldiers: Wallis was now at Shanagarry, Captain Bent at Carrigacotta and Saunders was still renting the remains of Castlemartyr from the state. Confiscation and transplantation were transforming the country.

The transition however worked well for Broghill. He was appointed lord president of Munster by the interim Council of State and once Charles II was restored to the throne Broghill was created Earl of Orrery. He was given a military commission, made one of the lords justices, and given lands in County Clare and financial rewards, although these were slow to be paid. In 1665 he was also given Castlemartyr.[2] Saunders' lease had not protected him although he eventually got a grant of land elsewhere. The late Earl of Cork had set himself up in west Waterford on Raleigh's fine estate but now the Boyle interest crossed the Blackwater as Orrery acquired substantial lands in east Cork.

Gone was his pleasure in simple living; now he had the positions he had coveted for so long he was keen to live in what he considered the appropriate style. To suit his position as lord president of Munster he quickly began work on a vast mansion in north Cork, at the centre of the presidential territory, which he named Charleville House. It cost him £20,000 which he could ill afford but the Earl of Orrery was extravagant. Yet, throughout the 1660s he or his countess were often in residence at Ballymaloe. They clearly liked it; it was not as grand and expensive as Charleville but Ballymaloe was convenient for Cork city and the coast.

---

[1] P. Little, *Lord Broghill and the Cromwellian Union*, (Woodbridge, 2004), p. 169.
[2] *The 56th Report of the Deputy Keeper of the Public Records of Ireland* (Dublin, 1928–62), p. 207.

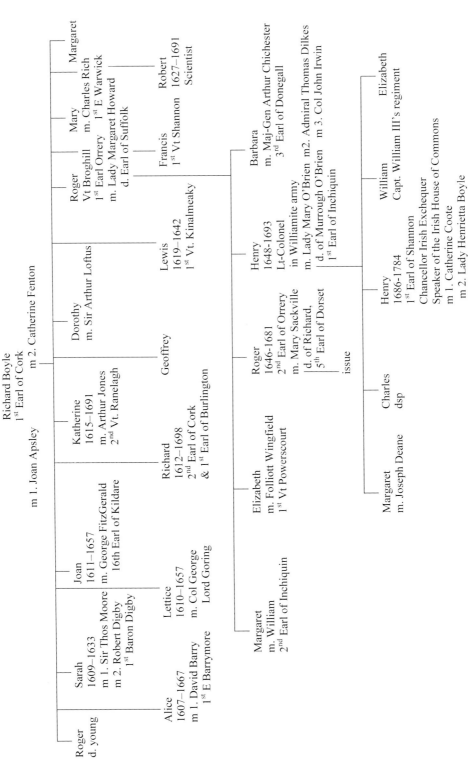

Orrery Family Tree.

7.   Cloyne Cathedral.

8.   Barryscourt Castle, a restored tower house.

9. The gargoyle on the turret.

10. The stairs within the turret.

12.	*The gate house from within the yard.*

11.	*Chamber within the turret.*

13.	*The gate house from without.*

14. *Charles Blount, 8ᵗʰ Baron Mountjoy, Lord Deputy of Ireland.*

© The Trustees of the British Museum

15. *Sir John FitzEdmund FitzGerald's carved stone at Ballymaloe House.*

16. *Sir John FitzEdmund's stone on the arch at Ballymaloe.*

17. *Sir John FitzEdmund's stone at Cloyne House*

*18.   Map of Imokilly, made for George Carew, Lord President of Munster,
early seventeenth century.*

By permission of The Board of Trinity College Dublin.

*19.   The FitzGerald Harp, replica
at Ballymaloe House.*

20. *The statue of the Virgin in the silver gilt shrine given by Lady Honora FitzGerald, St Mary's Church, Pope's Quay, Cork.*

21. *Earl of Castlehaven. Possibly James Touchet, 3rd Earl of Castlehaven attributed to Sir Peter Lely, oil on canvas, circa 1640s.*

Photograph, National Portrait Gallery, London, unknown collection.

22. *Murrough O'Brien, 1st Earl of Inchiquin, by John Michael Wright.*

By kind permission of Manchester Art Gallery.

Roger Boyle, y first Earl of Orrery: 1660.

23. *Roger Boyle, 1ˢᵗ Earl of Orrery, after a portrait of 1660 (engraving), English School, (seventeenth century).*

Private Collection / Bridgeman Images.

Lady Margaret Howard
wife of Roger 1ˢᵗ Earl of Orrery

24. *Margaret, Countess of Orrery.*

By permission of Mary Evans Picture Library.

25. *Portrait of Lady Mary Boyle, wife of Colonel Henry Boyle, with her son Charles Boyle, by Sir Godfrey Kneller.*

Private Collection. © Lawrence Steigrad Fine Arts, New York / Bridgeman Images

26. *Colonel Henry Boyle.*

By kind permission of Harry Boyle, 10th Earl of Shannon.

27. *Sir Thomas Dilkes.*

© National Maritime Museum, Greenwich, London, Greenwich Hospital Collection.

28. *The Queen Anne wing from the stable yard.*

29. *The Queen Anne wing from the front of the house.*

30.   The archway from within the yard and without.

31.   Colonel Corker's carved stone in the apex of the arch.

32.   The front entrance to the courtyard.

33.   The cellar showing the rocky outcrop.

34. *Portrait of Chuffe by J. Flynn at Ballymaloe.*

35. *The Jester, painting at Ballymaloe.*

36.   Map of Ballymaloe townland, from Griffiths Valuation 1845–1864.

Ordnance Survey, Ireland

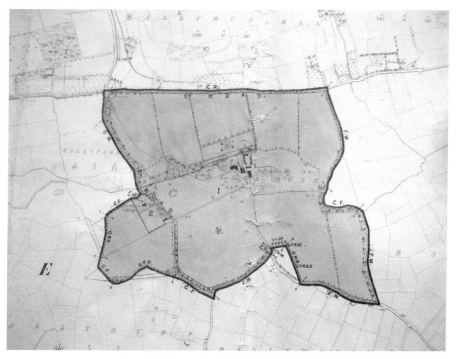

37.   Map of Ballymaloe from the sale particulars of 1883.

39.   Portrait of a Litchfield daughter.

38.   Portrait of a Litchfield son.

40.   Embroidered bodice belonging to the Litchfields.

41.   Butter pats used by Helen Morgan (née Simpson) as a girl.

42.   *Charles Simpson with Dorothy on the bridge over the River Rooskah behind Ballymaloe.*

43.   *Outside the main entrance looking down the road to Cloyne.*

44.   *Larry Neill the coachman in the yard.*

45.　*Ballymaloe House from the west.*

46.　*Harvesting.*

47.　*The pony trap coming up the drive.*

48.　*Bill Neill in the farmyard.*

There are few portraits of Orrery, but according to his biographer, 'his person was of a middle size, well-shaped and comely; his eyes had that Life and Quickness in them, which is usually the sign of great and uncommon parts. His Wit, his knowledge of the World, and his learning, rendered his conversation highly entertaining and instructive.'[3] No-one doubted Orrery's wits but he was ambitious and impatient and many thought him 'fickle and false', the 'Charlatan of Munster'.[4] The king saw him often, creating jealousy in the other courtiers, but Charles II liked to know what Orrery was thinking.

The earl travelled a great deal, to London where he sat in the House of Commons, and to Dublin on official business where he rented a house. Once Charleville was finished it became his country mansion and he kept his presidential court there, but nonetheless the Orrerys were at Ballymaloe in 1665 and 1668. In between they let it. One of the officers from his troop of horse, Captain George Dillon, wanted it in 1664 if he could have a lease for eleven years, but this was not agreed and Dillon was awarded land in Kerry when the settlements were made.[5] Soldiers were being settled, but the grants were constantly revised and people were moved – often several times. The royalists had returned too, anxious to reclaim their property.

Orrery was at work on the Act of Settlement himself, and is said to have written the preamble. The king said that 'the earl is too busy with the public settlement of Ireland to attend to his private estate', but people thought he had paid close attention; he and his brother both doubled their acres.[6]

Meanwhile Edmund FitzGerald was doing everything he could to get back Ballymaloe and as much as possible of his father's estate. He was acknowledged to have served the king; Lord Inchiquin, who was back in Ireland and in favour with the Crown, testified to FitzGerald's loyalty; a king's letter was sent to the lords justices stating, 'He shall be restored to the lands of which he was deprived by the late usurped power'[7] and FitzGerald was named in the Declaration of Thanks. But despite the declarations in Edmond's favour, there were two obstacles to him repossessing his estate. The first was a common problem after the Restoration: the lands had been given to others and in this case Orrery, a powerful politician, was in possession of Ballymaloe. The other problem was that the bishop had launched

---

3   E. Budgell, *Memoirs of the Lives and Characters of the Illustrious Family of the Boyles* (Dublin, 1737), p. 118.

4   Little, *Lord Broghill*, p. 236.

5   Bod. Lib. Carte Ms. 60, f. 551, Ms. 40, f. 648, Ms. 159, f. 79, Ms. 163, f. 12.

6   J. Ohlmeyer, *Making Ireland English* (New Haven, CT, 2012), pp. 317–18.

7   *CSPI, 1660–1662*, 31 Jan. 1661.

a new investigation into the Cloyne See lands and this time was so persistent that all the deceptions of the past were revealed.

There was a public enquiry in Cork in December 1664 at which commissioners called a Grand Jury to discover whether or not Sir John FitzGerald the younger had made a will. James the agent had died, but one of the witnesses to the signing at Ballyhonock was still alive, aged eighty. He told the story of Sir John Óg warming his hands on the bullet in order to sign the codicil. James the agent's grandson John FitzGerald gave rather damning testimony. He described how, ten years earlier when his grandfather was seriously ill in bed, he called the young man in, gave him a key and told him to open a box or small trunk in which Sir John's will was stored. James, who was dying, left a curse on his grandson if he did not divulge the will and restore the several forged and invented papers to the persons whose lands were detained, for, said he, 'there was never the like unjust things done since the creation of the world'. According to his grandson, the old man beat his breast and said he was damned, 'unless God be merciful to me, for these unjust dealings'.[8]

Land acts were being drafted, land was already being traded and the bishop was anxious to press his case before it was too late. He put pressure on Ormond, the lord lieutenant. 'There is nothing more notoriously known,' he told him, 'than that ye whole Bishopric of Cloyne and the lands belonging to it … was sacrilegiously swallowed upp by Sir John FitzEdmund Gerald of Ballymaloe and a great part of them still kept away from the church by his heirs.' He recounted the grand jury's findings at the King's Castle in Cork and the scandal of the concealed wills but he said that Mr FitzGerald had been making allegations and preventing the bishop defending the rights of the Church, 'Mr FitzGerald being now hovering at court waiting an opportunity to prejudice me'.[9]

Edmund FitzGerald was certainly doing everything he could to get back his estate. The outcome of the Act of Settlement often depended on who the claimants knew and what pressure could be brought to bear. Edmund petitioned Ormond and contacted any influential courtiers who might intercede for him. Among Ormond's papers are memos instructing his staff to follow up the claims and, if true, to restore the land, but as regards Ballymaloe, Orrery's position was too strong. The bishop too had a strong legal claim and Lord Inchiquin now held land in Imokilly which was also part of the dispute.[10]

---

[8]　Records of the See of Cloyne exhibited by Richard Caulfield and recorded in *Journal of the Royal Historical and Archaeological Association of Ireland*, vol. V, 1880, pp. 269–73.

[9]　Carte Ms. 45, f. 167, Cork, 5 June 1665.

[10]　Carte Ms. 145, f. 208.

Bishop Synge was successful and when the subsequent Act of Explanation was passed, Cloyne Castle and 600 acres along with Ballycotton were confirmed to the Church. Of the Church lands, Edmund FitzGerald was only awarded the remainder of the old lease.[11] There were thirty years to run on it but all the lands had been given to others. Despite further appeals, FitzGerald lost all his ancestor's land in Imokilly and after Charles II's reign, all such appeals ceased – the land settlement became final. By the same acts all of Orrery's land was confirmed to him and his title was secure.[12]

Edmund FitzGerald's line did not entirely disappear from east Cork as one of his descendants married into Inchiquin's family, but as a power in east Cork the time of the FitzGeralds was over. By the nineteenth century the Geraldines had emerged as nationalist heroes and Thomas Davis wrote a poem of praise for them:

The Geraldines! The Geraldines! – 'tis true, in Strongbow's van,
By lawless force, as conquerors, their Irish reign began;
And, oh! through many a dark campaign they proved their prowess stern,
In Leinster's plains, and Munster's vales, on king, and chief, and kerne;
But noble was the cheer within the halls so rudely won,
And generous was the steel-gloved hand that had such slaughter done;
How gay their laugh, how proud their mien, you'd ask no herald's sign –
Among a thousand you had known the princely Geraldine.

These Geraldines! These Geraldines! – not long our air they breathed;
Not long they fed on venison, in Irish water seethed
Not often had their children been by Irish mothers nursed
When from their full and genial hearts an Irish feeling burst!
The English monarchs strove in vain, by law, and force, and bribe,
To win from Irish thoughts and ways this 'more than Irish' tribe,
For still they clung to fosterage, to *breitheamh*, cloak, and bard
What king dare say to Geraldine, 'Your Irish wife discard'?[13]

The FitzGeralds however had lost their hold on Imokilly and the bishop had regained his lands and palace. It was this building in which Bishop Berkeley the

---

[11] Brady, *Clerical and Parochial*, vol. III (London, 1864), pp. 8–9; *The Irish Statutes from Edward II to the Union, 1310–1800* (Dublin, 1995), pp. 247–8.

[12] K.M. Lynch, 'Roger Boyle, First Earl of Orrery' (Knoxville, 1965), p. 124.

[13] T.O. Davis, *The Geraldines*, verses 2 & 3, from ucc.ie electronic texts. *Breitheamh* is a judge, referring to the Irish brehon law.

philosopher lived in the eighteenth century when he was a benign presence and improving landlord.

The Cromwellian war had left the Protestants ascendant. As one of their leaders, Orrery had a new estate and was a powerful politician; but he also had political enemies and in 1666 he was impeached in the London House of Commons. One of the charges was that he had used armed force to expel Edmund FitzGerald of Cloyne from Rostellan. Orrery replied that he was executing a legal process and that FitzGerald was attainted of murder, robbery and treason, and was a notorious papist. The impeachment failed.[14] Rostellan was now the home of Lord Inchiquin, who after an anguished period in exile had become a Catholic, returned at the Restoration and been magnificently rewarded in Irish land.

During the 1660s the Orrerys or their family were often at Ballymaloe; Orrery himself, his countess Margaret or his married daughter Elizabeth. The countess was a capable woman, more than a match for her energetic husband but more level-headed. They had married just before the war and had come to Ireland as the rebellion broke out when Lord Cork had reported, 'my daughter Broghill is so great with child, and full of spirit, as she resolves to bide out the brunt of these wars', while all the other women were leaving for England – Margaret was not easily afraid. She had been born Lady Margaret Howard, daughter of the Earl of Suffolk. She insisted on managing her own money, which was as well for her since Orrery spent lavishly and far beyond his means. His chaplain complimented Margaret for her 'piety, prudence and reserve', said she was 'beautiful in her person, very moderate in her expenses, and plain in her garb, serious and decent in her behaviour, careful in her family and tender of her lord'.[15] The Boyles had a Puritan outlook; Orrery's sister was a friend of Milton and the 1st Earl of Cork was the epitome of the Puritan work ethic, but Roger and Margaret combined it with Restoration opulence, which created a dynamic effect. They also had a property in Somerset, left to them by Orrery's father, which gave them a base in Britain.

They had two sons and three daughters when they moved to Ballymaloe; the eldest was Elizabeth, then Margaret, Roger and Henry – all in their teens, Katherine the youngest. But the countess became pregnant again after they came back to County Cork and had another daughter, Barbara, born in 1662 when Lady Orrery was thirty-nine.

The Orrerys moved in aristocratic circles. Orrery's father had made a place for himself among the nobility of both England and Ireland and had married his children into it. Orrery and his countess moved easily among the Restoration

---

[14] R. Bagwell, *Ireland under the Stuarts,* vol. III (London, 1916), p. 98.
[15] Quoted in Ohlmeyer, *Making Ireland English*, pp. 173–4.

elite. As they shifted residence from London to Somerset, to Ballymaloe, Dublin and most of all to Charleville, they kept up their accustomed splendour. Some of their household goods would move with them, as well as the key members of staff. Descriptions of the lavish furnishings at Charleville give a taste of the interior of Ballymaloe when they were in residence. 'Serge curtains and counterpane, curtains and valance with gilt leather fringe, grey serge bed with hangings, arras hangings, Indian taffeta' were used in interiors lush with heavy curtains and upholstery. They owned silver in profusion; plates, boxes for sugar, pepper and mustard, tankards and cups. The tables glittered with all the polished metal as guests assembled. Once Charleville was built, and subsequently when they rebuilt Castlemartyr, Ballymaloe was not a principal residence but even as an occasional home the style would be maintained.

They had large numbers of household servants who kept the houses running and prepared the splendid meals. When they were in Imokilly fish was bought from Ballycotton Bay and meat at market. Merchants in Cork and Youghal supplied sugar, anchovies and capers, hogsheads of claret and pipes of canary. The Orrerys had their own baker and could eat much of their own produce grown on their land. Their horses were both essential and highly prized; the grooms were important members of staff.[16]

Property needed maintenance, especially after a damaging war and a decade of neglect. Sir John Broderick, based near Midleton, looked after the Boyle estate for a time and told Orrery, 'so soon as the slater hath done at Ballymalowe he goes to Itermurrough where I fear last night's storm hath given him more work'.[17]

His property and lifestyle were lavish and Orrery had financial problems. The grandeur of his multiple homes was far too expensive for his real income. His large landed estate was tenanted and he soon looked for tenants for Ballymaloe. He had been guardian to a wealthy young man named Folliott Wingfield who married Orrery's eldest daughter Elizabeth in the year of the Restoration. The title Lord Powerscourt was revived for Wingfield and the young couple set about rebuilding the mansion of Powerscourt as their home. While this was underway Folliott and Elizabeth took a tenancy of Ballymaloe from her father and were there for about five years. This was convenient; Lord Powerscourt was well-off and could afford the house but the family could still visit Elizabeth at Ballymaloe. The countess would stay with her daughter; Cooper the agent wrote to her there on estate matters, but early in 1669 Cooper let the earl know that 'Lady Powerscourt having decided to make Powerscourt her sole place of residence wishes to resign

---

[16] T.C. Barnard, *Irish Protestant Ascents and Descents* (Dublin, 2004), pp. 53–5, 67.
[17] E. MacLysaght, *Calendar of Orrery Papers* (Dublin, 1941), p. 56.

her interest in Ballymaloe as soon as a satisfactory tenant for it is found'.[18]

After that we hear no more of the Orrerys at Ballymaloe. The earl lost his job as president of Munster in 1672 so they left Charleville and moved to Castlemartyr which they had rebuilt and refurbished. Their wayward eldest son and his wife moved into Charleville while the earl and countess set about improving the house and gardens at Castlemartyr.

Orrery had been given the right to erect a borough and manor at Castlemartyr, which increased his legal rights over his estate. The manor included Castlemartyr itself, Ballymaloe, Ightermurragh, Carew's Wood and thirty-nine other townlands in County Cork.[19]

The land at Ballymaloe was let to William FitzGerald, dean of Cloyne, who was from the Kerry family and a Protestant. His rent was £25 for a half year but he fell into arrears. Orrery had quit rent – a government tax – to pay on all his land grants; Ballymaloe cost 18s 6d a year in tax; which with hearth tax made owning property expensive.[20] Tenants were not so easy to find in the aftermath of war with its radical upheavals; gaps between tenants weakened Orrery's finances further.

The soldiers of the Civil War did not live to be old; Orrery died in 1679 aged fifty-five. His old protagonist Inchiquin died before him. However, after decades of family rivalry, their children had married. A match had been arranged between Inchiquin's eldest son William Lord O'Brien and Lady Margaret Boyle.

The close relationship between the two families soon led to a second wedding. Orrery's second son Henry, 'an accomplished gentleman, but more the soldier than the scholar', was as steady and reliable as his elder brother was profligate. Henry was a captain in the army and was later promoted to lieutenant colonel.[21] 'The Colonel fell in love with the Lady Mary O'Brien, daughter to Murrough Earl of Inchiquin. They made up a match, where love and inclination were only concerned and were marr'd on the Battlements of Limerick,' the ancestral seat of the mighty O'Briens – or so a later biographer tells us.[22] They made a good match, Henry Boyle was blond and well-honed, Mary O'Brien was dark and buxom with much of her father's glamour. Henry was also attentive to estate matters and frequently wrote to his parents on family issues. The great house at Charleville was to go to the eldest son, but when Orrery made his will he

---

[18] Ibid., pp. 39–40, 56, 65–6.
[19] National Archives of Ireland, Ms. 2449, No. 12.
[20] Petworth House, *Orrery Papers*, Ms. 13,177, Ms. 13,193.
[21] T. Morrice (ed.), *A Collection of State Letters of Orrery* (Dublin, 1743), p. 50.
[22] E. Budgell, *An Account of the Life, Character and Parliamentary Conduct of the Rt. Hon. Henry Boyle Esq.*, (Dublin, 1754), p. 12.

left Castlemartyr for the use of Margaret his countess for her lifetime, while the whole of his Imokilly estate went to his son Henry, who became the new owner of Ballymaloe.[23]

After her husband's death, Margaret the dowager countess did not stay long in Ireland but went to live with her sister the Duchess of Northumberland in England. Since she had no need of Castlemartyr, Henry settled there with his wife Lady Mary and their children.

There was probably a tenant at Ballymaloe but no records have as yet come to light. If so, it was surely another soldier but the tenancies may have been short in case the family wanted to live there again. Castlemartyr was now Colonel Henry's main residence but Ballymaloe might have been intended as a dower house for his family; certainly his widow had legal rights over it as we shall see.

After James II fled England, the situation swiftly changed. Henry Boyle wrote to his mother in February 1689 that 'The whole county of Kerry and all westward of Bandon that belonged to the English all destroyed.' As a Protestant and a soldier, he gathered about 140 gentry and servants at Castlemartyr to defend it for King William but sent his wife and children to England, writing to his mother that 'all the towns and villages are full of soldiers'.[24] Despite his efforts, Justin MacCarthy besieged Castlemartyr and Henry surrendered on terms. He was taken prisoner to Cork but escaped and joined his regiment in England. Henry returned to Ireland with King William and fought at the Boyne.[25] In 1690 Castlemartyr was the scene of more intense fighting and when Henry regained his property later that year 'Castlemartyr, with all the improvements and furniture, to the value of some thousands of pounds, were destroyed.'[26]

The FitzGeralds had not entirely given up their claims. A judgement was given in 1690 in which Colonel Henry Boyle stated that Captain Edmond FitzGerald had been aiding and assisting in rebellion against His Majesty and that fifteen properties in Imokilly and Barrymore were likely to go to ruin, and so to save them from further harm Colonel Henry wanted to possess them on behalf of the Crown, notwithstanding any former grants to other people. The order was in Colonel Henry's favour.

We hear nothing of Ballymaloe during the Williamite war, despite the intense

---

[23] MacLysaght, *Calendar of Orrery Papers*, p. 222.

[24] Ibid., p. 369.

[25] D. Dickson, *Old World Colony* (Cork, 2005), p. 56; A. Collins, *The Peerage of England* (London, 1768), p. 157.

[26] Smith, *Antient and Present … Cork*, vol. II, p. 197; S. Hayman, *Annals of Youghal* (Youghal, 1848), p. 56.

fighting by Marlborough in Cork and Schomberg's campaign in the county. Henry Boyle did not survive this war for long. His regiment was put under Schomberg's command and they were sent to Flanders where Henry was killed in 1693. Lady Mary became a widow with six young children and may well have lived at Ballymaloe while Castlemartyr was rebuilt. She had to keep up the Imokilly estate which was to be her son's inheritance.

Lady Mary was a gallant woman, the daughter of Inchiquin and his half-Dutch wife. She had her mother's tenacity and her father's courage. With the help of her family and her agent, she had Castlemartyr rebuilt and was there on Christmas Day 1703. By then she had remarried and was the wife of Sir Thomas Dilkes, an admiral in the Royal Navy. She wrote to Southwell on that Christmas Day, 'My spouse is ordered to the Downs, so that I think it is but reasonable I should go to him, and in order to it, beg you wold let me know if any ship goes from these ports.'[27] The wars had begun by which France and Britain would contest for power. They would enrich Cork and this wealth would wash into Ballymaloe, but they also made shipping extremely hazardous. Lady Mary was unafraid.

Richard Waller was now the tenant at Ballymaloe. His ancestor had come to Ireland as a soldier of fortune in the parliamentarian army in 1641 soon after the rebellion and eventually been rewarded with an estate in Tipperary, later called Castle Waller. Soldiers and the sons of soldiers were still trying to settle themselves but claims, counter-claims and legal complexities dogged them – many had sold up. At least the Boyles had a tenant.

Lady Mary's second husband died while away at sea in 1707 and she remarried: her third husband was Colonel John Irwin of Tanrago, County Sligo, who was twenty years younger than her. Despite the age difference, Lady Mary brought prestige to her young husband. He often had the harper Turlough O'Carolan at his house, who composed a famous piece for his host named 'Colonel John Irwin'.

Lady Mary's eldest son Roger died very young so the heir to Ballymaloe was the second son, Henry, born in 1686. He was grown up and had become MP for Midleton when he and his mother signed a lease for Ballymaloe to a man named Edward Corker. The year was 1709 and the lease was for perpetual renewal.[28] Although the Boyles would own Ballymaloe until late in the nineteenth century, none of them lived in it again. The time of the soldier was coming to an end; the time of the politicians and merchants was beginning.

---

[27] T. Thorpe, *Thomas Thorpe's Catalogue of Books* (Oxford, 1839).
[28] Registry of Deeds, Book 9, p. 4, no. 2899.

CHAPTER TEN

Colonel Edward Corker

A new civil service gave employment to many ex-soldiers, including Edward Corker of Ratoath in County Louth who got several good jobs. Through his contacts his nephew, also Edward Corker, moved south, took a lease on Ballymaloe and became an MP for a Cork constituency.

The Corkers came from Lancashire; but two members of the family served in Ireland under Charles I's standard during the War of Three Kingdoms. Edward the uncle was a professional soldier and served in an infantry regiment in King William's army which fought in Ireland in 1689 and subsequently in Belgium in 1695.[1] Corker settled in Louth and had an influential job as commissioner for forfeited estates; in fact he caused considerable problems for the Boyles by the way he apportioned charges on their lands.[2] He then became agent to the Duke of Ormond, working with Sir Richard Cox of Cork and through this connection the Corkers too came south to Munster.[3]

The soldiers of the two wars formed a social circle in which royalists and Cromwellians began to blend. Uncle Corker had gone into business with Waller, an ex-soldier, attempting to set up the first sugar manufactory in Ireland.[4] The nephew too moved in these circles.

Edward Corker the nephew may have served in King William's army when he was young and was often known as colonel, but his only service record is in the Cork Militia Dragoons when he was in his late forties. In 1701, when he was twenty-one, he married Margaret Wallis who came from County Cork. Her

---

[1] J. O'Hart, *The Irish Landed Gentry* (Dublin, 1969), p. 387; C. Dalton, *English Army Lists*, vol. IV (London, 1898), p. 31.

[2] *Calendar of Treasury Books* (London, 1933), vol. 12, p. 131.

[3] T.C. Barnard, *A New Anatomy of Ireland* (New Haven, CT, 2003), p. 214; T.C. Barnard and J. Fenlon (eds), *The Dukes of Ormonde* (Woodbridge, 2000), pp. 216–17, 241.

[4] *CSPI, 1666–1669*, 3 Jan. 1668, p. 561.

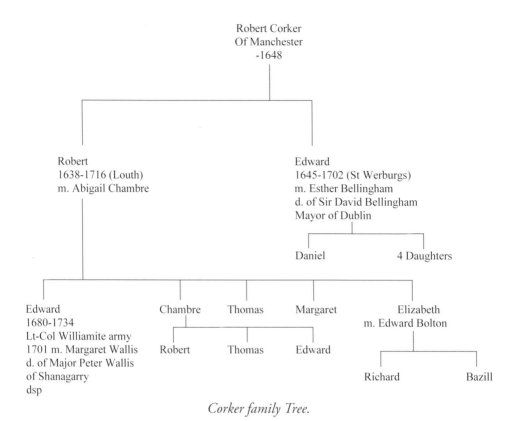

Corker family Tree.

father was the same Colonel Peter Wallis who had been both a parliamentarian and Cromwellian soldier, and had briefly rented Ballymaloe. Wallis had been awarded the land and castle at Shanagarry but after the Restoration the settlement had been revised and Shanagarry given to Admiral William Penn. When the admiral's son William came to east Cork in 1667 to sort out his father's land grant, Peter Wallis was still at Shanagarry, although he had to give it up. William Penn the younger had only recently become a Quaker and his diary records the meetings and prayer sessions among the houses of east Cork. 'I spoke in the power of the Lord God a few words to backsliders,' Penn wrote of one such meeting, and of another that 'it was a most precious meeting'.[5] These short extracts give a flavour of the Quaker meetings to which Peter Wallis belonged. His daughter had been brought up among these religious radicals but by the end of the century when Corker moved to Cork, the most intense and visionary moment had passed. It looks as though Margaret had moved back into the Church of Ireland. There

---

5   W. Penn, *My Irish Journal, 1669–1670*, edited by I. Grubb (London, 1952), pp. 28, 34.

are memorials for both Edward and Margaret Corker in Church of Ireland churches and Edward Corker's relatives were clergymen in the established church.

Patronage by the great was key to a man's career and uncle Corker was well-connected. His nephew took the lease on Ballymaloe in 1709 and four years later he got a seat in parliament for Rathcormack. In the parliament of 1715 he was MP for Midleton which had a new charter giving it two MPs and was then under the patronage of the Broderick family of Ballyannan.[6] Corker held this seat for a decade. In parliament he was a Whig, sat on several committees and voted twice against the creation of a national bank. He was also High Sheriff of County Cork in 1719.

Margaret's father Peter Wallis had lost the lands at Shanagarry to William Penn who also owned Ballymaloebegg, the lower part of Ballymaloe to the south of the Shanagarry road.[7] Wallis had died in 1679 and Margaret's brother had moved to their mother's property at Carrigrohane, the other side of Cork city.[8] Margaret stayed in east Cork where she had grown up and was mistress of Ballymaloe for twelve years.

When they took the lease, Edward and Margaret clearly intended to stay and make a family home. The Corkers made substantial changes to the house; they added a new wing which altered the orientation of the house. The position of the wing was defined by the ground levels and the existing gable end of the Jacobean house. Corker built on from the end of this gable wall to create a new structure at right angles to the main house, creating an L-shaped mansion of two almost separate parts and with a new staircase in the corner of the L. The gable wall was extended to become the side of the new staircase which had windows only to the south.

The entrance arch to the east dates from this phase of building. It is later than the gatehouse as its construction blocks arrow-slits in the side of that small building. The gatehouse was probably remodelled; it had been higher. Like old Sir John before him, Edward Corker put up a carved stone with his initials and the date 1709. It was embedded into the apex of the arch, whereas one of Sir John's stones was left at the side of the arch, which gave Corker the ascendant position.

The new wing was in the Queen Anne style and built of brick. It was three storeys under a slate roof, with slightly protruding brick courses to break up the façade and decorate it. The new wing faced east and west, which was popular at the time as the sun did less damage to the fabrics which were used for upholstery

---

[6]   E.M. Johnston-Liik, *History of the Irish Parliament, 1692–1800*, vol. III, (Belfast, 2002), p. 509; S. Lewis, *A Topographical Dictionary of Ireland*, vol. II (London, 1837), p. 369.

[7]   Penn, *My Irish Journal*, pp. 95–6.

[8]   B. Burke, *Burke's Irish Family Records* (Buckingham, 2007), p. 1,184.

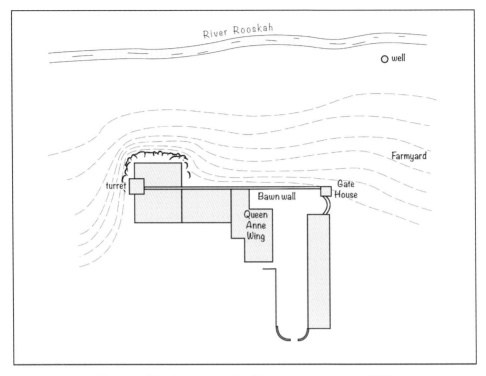

Plan 3.   The house with the Queen Anne wing, c. 1709.

and sometimes as curtains; the damask, wool and velvet fabrics were vulnerable
to south-facing houses with bright sun. The wing had an additional rectangular
structure in which the new staircase was constructed. Attached at right angles
to the Jacobean house, the new wing altered the eastern entrance of Ballymaloe.
The yard was clearly reshaped at the same time and the second opening to the
south, with its stone gateposts topped with balls, created a smart entrance for
riders. Ladies might be driven up to the south-facing door of the Jacobean house
but gentlemen might ride into the courtyard and here give their horses to the
grooms to be stabled.

   Entering the house from this side, visitors came into a stone-flagged hallway
which in turn led to the new staircase. There was a clear view of the archway from
the stone hall which now became central to the house. From this hall you could
go straight on into the Jacobean house, turn left into the new reception room on
the ground floor of the wing, or mount the new staircase with its fine newel posts
and hand-rails. Lit by south-facing windows, the staircase rose to the panelled
chambers above. From these upper rooms there was a view of the parkland to
the south-west and across the farm to the east. From the first-floor landing it was
possible to walk through into the bedchambers of the earlier house.

Many of the window openings in the wing are blocked now. This may have been done to avoid hearth tax but as this was not high or well-collected, it is more likely that the windows were blocked from the beginning; otherwise the rooms would be too cold and have no wall surface for cupboards and furniture.[9]

Corker's brother-in-law Peter Foulkes was his business partner when they rented a large part of the Penn estate in Imokilly, consisting of 100 messuages, 200 cottages, 100 gardens, 10 orchards, 3 mills, 2 pigeon houses, 1,000 acres of land, 200 acres of meadow, 1,000 acres of pasture, 500 acres of woodland and 400 acres of moor, marsh and heath in Shanagarry, Kilmahon and other parishes, all in Imokilly.[10] An agreement had been signed but it took several court judgements before Penn honoured it; when he did, Edward Corker acknowledged it by the gift of a sparrowhawk. Some of this property was sub-let but Corker and Foulkes may well have had a livestock business of their own.

Edward and Margaret had no descendants. One pedigree records a son who married in the year of Edward's death but all the other records show they had no children.[11] The only small person at Ballymaloe was Chuffe the dwarf, who was a household pet. He was said to be the illegitimate child of Edward Corker but whether this was true or not, Margaret was fond of him and treated him kindly. The maids teased him because of his small stature but he was an important member of the household. Colonel Corker liked country sports; he enjoyed fishing and went out with his neighbours to shoot pheasants and other game. Accidents with shotguns are not uncommon and poor Chuffe was peppered with shot.

His portrait hangs in the drawing room at Ballymaloe House with a poem about him. They tell how 'to please a good mistress' Chuffe had been drawn 'as you see', but how the 'maids won't allow I'm a man'. The shooting accident had left shot in Chuffe's body which had never been removed; since 'a brace of hard balls in my body still be, that will ever disquiet my rest'. His father is given as Richard 'Noonane', meaning he was illegitimate. When Chuffe died he was buried just outside the castle on the north side where a stone once marked his grave, but which is now under the floor of the cellar.

The portrait of the jester in the drawing room is from the same period. Colonel Corker seems a gruff military man who enjoyed country sports, but there was entertainment in the house at which the jester performed so it cannot have been a Puritan household. Margaret managed the staff, was kind to Chuffe and seems to have been a gentle presence in the household.

---

[9] Most of the detail on the wing was kindly contributed by Frank Keohane.
[10] Cork City and County Archives, U229/172/2; U229/143/3g; U229/143/3d.
[11] Johnston-Liik, *History of the Irish Parliament*, vol. III, p. 509.

Edward Corker was both a tenant of the Boyles at Castlemartyr and a fellow MP. Colonel Henry and Lady Mary Boyle's son Henry was now the head of the household at Castlemartyr and MP for County Cork, advancing quickly in a high-flying career. He and Corker were on good terms; Henry Boyle wrote to Edward Corker in the summer of 1728 saying how sorry he was not to have written sooner but he had been busy with tedious privy council business, otherwise 'I would not have kept silent so long, from returning my dear Corker a thousand thanks for ye fine fish which was with me last Sunday morning'. Boyle could not resist discussing parliamentary schemes, but he hoped 'for the pleasure of seeing you – I hope yr furniture for ye Castle rooms got home safe, I long to see where ye Chest stands, which I would soon do could I creep with sticks instead of a crutch, thank god I am very well, all to ye weakness in my ancles'. He ends, 'most sincerely and affectionately yours'.[12]

There was a portrait of Edward Corker at Ballymaloe then; when Charles Smith published his history in 1750 Corker's relatives in Cork still had it. He also had a library in the house because Smith had a copy of his bookplate with the Corker arms printed on it. They had been granted to his uncle in 1696.[13]

The Corkers were married for twenty years; Margaret died in 1721 and was buried with her aunt and sister at Cloyne cathedral; 'the dutiful, modest, learned and generous daughter of Peter Wallis' the inscription reads, 'dearly beloved wife' of Edward Corker who erected the monument.[14] He put up other and more emotional inscriptions. When his uncle died in 1702 a monument was erected in St Werburgh's Dublin with a Latin inscription which translates:

Close to here lies buried Edward Corker, Armig. A man who, if no body ever was, is worthy of eternal praise as a father, husband, brother and a most generous uncle and what sounds more loudly he was outstanding in his devotion towards God. There testifies to this amongst other things in the sight of all, the church in the village of Monkstown, which was rebuilt at his own personal expense. He was moreover most loving of his fatherland and likewise towards King William III, the father of his native land. He was always faithful in the various public offices in which he engaged and in the public assemblies of the kingdom. When he heard of his death and overcome

---

12   NLI, Shannon Papers, Ms. 13,296.

13   Smith, *Antient and Present … Cork*, vol. I, (1774), p. 108; Johnston-Liik, *Irish Parliament*, vol. III, p. 508.

14   R. Henchion, *The Graveyard Inscriptions of the Cathedral Cemetery of Cloyne, Co. Cork* (Midleton, 2001), p. 158.

with grief when he died on the 31ˢᵗ March 1702, his surviving nephew Edward Corker, Armig. of Ballymaloe, just a few days after receiving the grievous news, erected this to a most deserving and excellent uncle.[15]

He put up another long inscription to his mother and her Chambre relatives in County Louth which also ends Eduardus Corker de Ballymaloe Armiger/ Posuit. Armiger confirms that he was a soldier or military knight.

Edward had siblings; his brother Thomas was in Dublin while Chambre was in Cork, as was Margaret Corker; 'a Maiden lady and sister to the late worthy and renowned patriot Colonel Edward Corker of Ballymaloe' her death notice recited. The family were prominent in the Cork area for generations; Chambre's son Thomas lived at Lota House and his son the Rev. Chambre Corker was archdeacon of Ardagh.

A strange story was told of the Corkers by Gibson, the Cork historian. 'The family tomb is in Cloyne cathedral. A Miss Corker was buried here. When the tomb was opened some years ago, an orange silk handkerchief was found binding her brow; and I am credibly informed, by a lady, a near relative of the family, who saw the precious relic, that a guinea was freely given for a square inch or two of it.'[16]

Regarding his property, Corker was back in the old wrangle. The lawsuits over the bishop of Cloyne's land had not ended in Corker's lifetime. The sixty-year lease ran out just before Corker came to Imokilly, setting off more claims, while the complexity of the land settlements since that time and of the FitzGerald wills had not been entirely resolved. No-one challenged the Boyle ownership of Ballymaloe but much of the Imokilly settlement was still in dispute. The FitzGeralds had gone into the female line and married into the family of the Earl of Inchiquin who also had claims through his mother. Sir John Broderick and Colonel Corker both had lawsuits against the bishop of Cloyne, not only for land but also a mill, while market and other rights were in contention. Bishop Pooley hardly had the income to fight these legal battles but he did protest energetically against Colonel Corker cutting turf in his bog.[17]

Edward Corker died in 1734 and leaving no descendants, he made a will in favour of his brothers and nephews. His brother Thomas, a merchant in Dublin, was executor and within three months he had sold the lease of Ballymaloe together with the furniture and the inventory of lime, timber and other materials to Hugh

---

[15] In Latin, Brady, *Clerical and Parochial*, vol. III (London, 1864), p. 169, for translation, Henchion, *Graveyard Inscriptions … Cloyne*, p. 159.

[16] C.B. Gibson, *The History of the County and City of Cork*, vol. 2 (London, 1861), p. 447.

[17] Brady, *Clerical and Parochial*, vol. II, p. 6, vol. III, pp. 11, 24.

Lumley for £2,100. Henry Boyle the owner was to renew the lease within six months.[18]

These leases were for three lives. Any life could be named; in some cases it was the king, but when any of the individuals died the lease had to be renewed and a fee paid to the owner. Rents could be increased on renewal but if the three lives were long and inflation high, rents sometimes got far behind current values. As long as the tenant fulfilled the terms of the lease they had a right of renewal in perpetuity. The purpose of these leases was to attract Protestant tenants who would settle long-term, since the Penal Laws prevented Catholic ones; but there were too few potential tenants. The leases were eventually altered by parliament during the great land upheavals of the nineteenth century, when property ownership in Ireland had to be unscrambled.

At Ballymaloe however a new proprietor rode into the stable yard to take possession of his fine house. Hugh Lumley made himself comfortable in the splendid old house and, as agreed, early the following year the 'Rt. Hon. Henry Boyle, Speaker of the House of Commons, Chancellor of His Majesties Court of Exchequer and one of His Majesties most honble. Privy Council in Ireland' signed a new lease to Hugh Lumley for Ballymalowmore and Parklylessig 'by common estimate containing one half a ploughland and ten Irish acres'. This was not the whole of the old Ballymaloe townland; it would take time and more indentures before the original lands were recollected to the house but it was a lease for 199 years at an annual rent of £30, with a £10 fee for renewal.[19]

Hugh Lumley looked out of the windows of Sir John FitzGerald's splendid house, climbed the stairs in Corker's new wing and surveyed the fine land of the Cloyne valley with the sun pouring in from the south. It was spring and he could not help but be pleased with his bargain.

---

[18] P.B. Eustace (ed.), *Registry of Deeds: Abstract of Wills* (Dublin, 1956); Cork City and County Archives, U229/172/2.

[19] Registry of Deeds, Book 76, p. 449. no. 55325.

CHAPTER ELEVEN

Gentlemen of Business

Mr Hugh Lumley

Hugh Lumley was not born in Ireland, nor born a Lumley. He was born Hugh Raincock in Penrith, Cumbria, in the north of England, but his great-uncle Henry had moved to Ireland and made Hugh his heir, asking that he change his name. So Hugh Raincock came to Cork, became Hugh Lumley and moved into Ballymaloe.[1]

The Lumleys came from Skelton, a small place on the edge of the Cumbrian hills. Henry Lumley retained property there all his life but moved to Ireland, while his sister Grace married John Raincock and moved to Penrith where Raincock went into business. Henry came to Ireland after the Restoration and invested in property. He also became comptroller of the customs in Cork in 1684, a highly advantageous job which suggests that he had connections.[2] It brought a good salary as well as business chances and commissions. It also threw him into the centre of the Cork business community. The corporation were keen to develop the city and the port was set for a century of swift expansion. The old city was walled and contained on its island, but the marsh and waste surrounding it was being reclaimed. Henry Lumley got possession of a slice of wasteland on the east marsh. When Huguenots fled to Cork from France, he rented them a piece of land on 'Lumley's Lane' to build a church. That lane is now French Church Street.[3]

Cork merchants had international connections, in Britain and far afield. Henry Lumley was very close to Cornelius Conner of Bandon who had built

---

[1] Cork City and County Archives, U681 52/17/31; *The Registers of the Parish Church of Skelton, Cumberland 1580–1812*, translated by H. Brierly (1918).

[2] J.L.J. Hughes (ed.), *Patentee Officers in Ireland, 1173–1824* (Dublin, 1960).

[3] G. Lawless, *The Huguenot Settlements in Ireland* (London, 1936), p. 40.

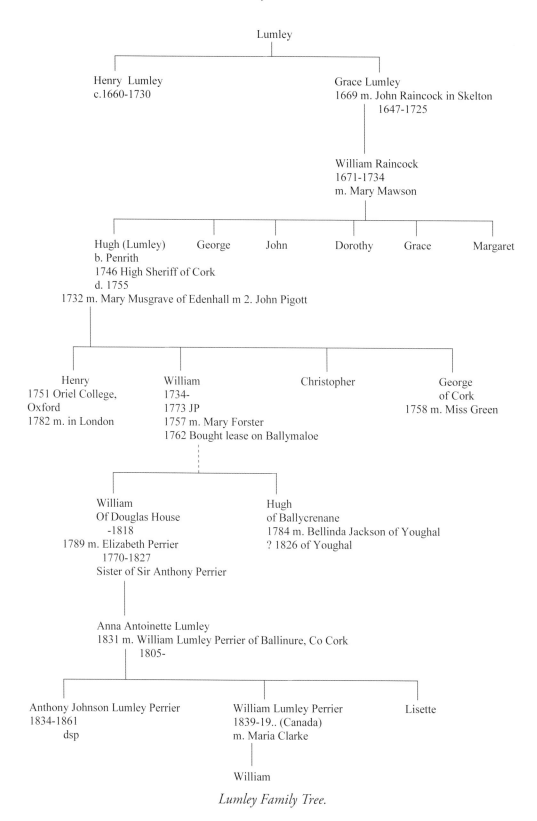

Lumley Family Tree.

up a shipping fortune in Bristol and referred to 'my good friend Henry Lumley' in his will.[4] Lumley also did property deals in north Cork with John Longfield who had a job as tax collector in Mallow and was also buying property. Lending money for interest, investing businesses by buying bonds, Lumley was a typical Cork businessman. In his dealings a pattern emerged which continued for over a century, where men of property took government jobs, bought leased and rented out land, lent money on mortgage and borrowed at interest while investing in the growing commerce of Cork, a burgeoning Atlantic port.

Henry was unmarried and childless. When he died in 1730 he was a wealthy man. He left generous bequests to all the Connor family and to his sister Grace Raincock's children who were merchants in Penrith and London. Henry left bequests to his nephew William Raincock as well as William's children, the eldest of whom was his principal heir. Henry's great-nephew Hugh now prepared to move to Ireland. Before he did so he married a girl from Cumbria, Mary Musgrave of Edenhall. Hugh had already been introduced to the Cork business community by his great-uncle and joined the Common Council of the Cork Corporation almost on arrival.[5] Once in Cork and established in business, he set himself up as a country gentleman by taking the lease of Ballymaloe.

Hugh's four sons were born in swift succession: Henry in 1733, then William, Christopher and lastly George in 1737. He sent his boys to university – Henry to Oxford and William to Trinity College, Dublin. Christopher began at Oxford but moved to Trinity. George the youngest went to Christ Church in Oxford.[6]

A fellow Cumbrian was also at Ballymaloe: John Seetree, who was involved in the Lumleys' property activities. They went to court in 1743 with Seetree taking a suit against Richard Burke of Dublin over property at Curryhally. Hugh Lumley was in court both as a witness and as a previous owner; Seetree had taken over the lease from him.[7] So it went on, the assignment and mortgage of property and the sub-letting, which was viable as the economy grew but was already building up a tangle of ownership and borrowings which one day would have to be resolved.

The Huguenot presence in Cork had grown, making a great contribution to Cork commercial life. Hugh Lumley leased a second property to them for an almshouse and his descendants married into one of the leading Huguenot families.

Hugh Lumley took the lease for Ballymaloe in 1734; he and Mary brought up their four sons in the house. There was a swift expansion of trade in

---

[4]   P.B. Eustace (ed.), *Registry of Deeds: Abstract of Wills* (Dublin, 1956), no. 192.

[5]   R. Caulfield, *The Council Book of the Corporation of Cork* (Guildford, 1876), p. 502.

[6]   *Alumni Dubliensis* (Dublin, 1935); *Alumni Oxonienses*, vol. 3, 1715–1886.

[7]   Cork City and County Archives, U681 52/17/26.

eighteenth-century Ireland, especially around the ports – Cork grew in size, population and wealth. Hugh's business prospered and as his sons were growing up he decided to enlarge and improve the house in the contemporary style. Corker had built to the east but the Lumleys built to the north. This meant extending down to the valley floor of the Rooskah.

The Lumleys hired a local architect, John Morrison of Midleton, who had been patronised by Lord Shannon of Castlemartyr and whose father was also an architect. Morrison had both mathematical and design skills, and he had plenty of opportunities in the boom years around Cork harbour which made his fortune.[8] Morrison added a large new structure which wrapped around the back of the Jacobean house. It created a new north façade for the house, a typical early Georgian one with three storeys, the windows decreasing in size from the ground floor to the top according to the classical pattern. In the centre a break-front protruded slightly – like the brick course of the wing, the slight interruption to the smooth façade improved the look of the design. Ballymaloe House is sited on a rock outcrop which curves, so the new structure enclosed the rock and created a cellar.

The house doubled in size, allowing the service rooms to be moved to the back and lower floor. The old curtain wall – running from turret to gatehouse – was no longer the back wall but buried within the house. The Georgian part had three floors over the basement but the Jacobean section had only two. The new structure created many new bedrooms for family and guests on the first floor, with room for a nursery and servants' quarters at the top as well.

Following the fashion of the time, ornamental gardens were laid out to the north of the house with a lake. Approaching the house from Castlemartyr, a visitor would come in at an angle so that the elegant new façade, set amid its park and pleasure gardens, would be visible from the carriage window. There was plenty of room to make a gravel carriage sweep on the north of the house and a fine curved opening was at the centre of the ground floor which would create a new front door. Steps rose from the carriage sweep to this new door which opened into a hallway leading to the reception rooms. Corker had entered from the east but Lumley made the entrance on the north while the main reception rooms faced south.

At some time in the eighteenth century Sir John's carved stone with its Tudor roses was moved from its place over the front door. If it was moved at this stage it would have been below the threshold of the curved opening, so perhaps the stone was moved in the next phase of building when the south façade too was remodelled.

_____

8   *Dictionary of Irish Architects* on www.dia.ie, Morrison.

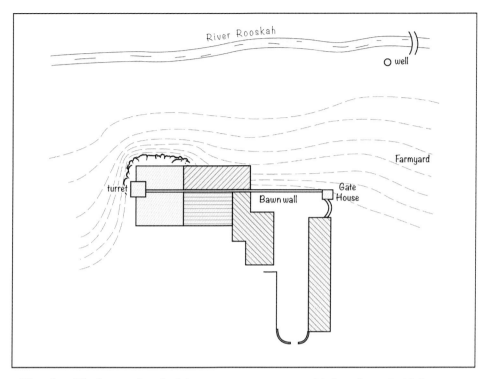

Plan 4.   The house after the Morrison extension was added in the early 18th century.

When Charles Smith wrote his history of Cork in the mid-eighteenth century the antlers of the giant deer, which had been found in Colonel Corker's day, were mounted in the hall. The painting of Chuffe was also in the hall, but the portrait of Corker had gone to his relatives in Cork.[9] Smith was impressed with the gardens and 'other plantations'. The walled garden dates from this time and was probably built when the house was enlarged. Hugh Lumley was particular about cider and had a new method – boiling before fermenting – which reduced the volume and made it stronger. Lumley had introduced arbutus or strawberry tree to the garden, an almond tree which bore fruit, the 'arbor vitae of Gerrard' and several kinds of myrtle which did well in the mild climate.

Hugh Lumley did not enjoy his fine new house for long; he was only fifty-five when he died in 1755. Two of his sons were still at university. His eldest son Henry took charge; it was he who put up the fine memorial for his father in Cloyne cathedral. This too was designed by Morrison. The memorial described Hugh Lumley as 'a brave and upright man of old-fashioned virtue who, although

---

[9]   Smith, *Antient and Present State of the County and City of Cork*, vol. I, p. 132.

born in England, was a true lover of this country'.[10] Henry was swift to set up an annuity for his mother in conformity with his father's will but she swiftly remarried, to a soldier named John Pigott. Henry took over Ballymaloe and carried on his father's property and business interests, but not with the same success. In 1762 he was sued by two separate parties, for £600 and £1,200 respectively. The family and business connection with the Connors of west Cork took a different turn when Henry sold property in Limerick and Cork to them for £5,670.[11] Either his wealth was contracting or he was preparing to move, but three years later he let Ballymaloe go by selling the lease to his brother William for £2,100. Henry moved to England where his father's family were in business and continued to unwind his Irish inheritance; he sold property in Muskerry to Richard Longfield.[12]

Richard Longfield lived at Castle Mary on the far side of Cloyne from Ballymaloe. He was a large landowner and ambitious politician. In fact, the three families, Lumley, Connor and Longfield, had done numerous business deals in the early years of the century and the two latter families intermarried many times. The world of the Munster Protestants was small.

When William Lumley took the lease of Ballymaloe from his elder brother, he was in business in Cork where he remained a merchant and official all his life. Soon after his father's death he married a girl named Mary Forster whose father Clement lived in Cloyne. Only a few years after the marriage, William had to go to his father-in-law for a mortgage of £1,000: this was the first indication of financial problems.[13] William and Mary Lumley had two sons, Hugh and William, but their affairs did not prosper. In 1772 the first deal was struck with Richard Longfield of Castle Mary.

Clement Forster had business dealings with Richard Longfield and it was to this prosperous landowner that the Lumleys turned. Longfield was increasing his property portfolio and he agreed to buy the head lease of Ballymaloe while retaining William Lumley as tenant. In 1772 the lease was assigned to Longfield for £600 and three years later a deed was signed for a further payment of £5,000.[14] The Lumleys still had the tenancy with a right to renew but the terms had changed, there was now an annual rent of £285, while Longfield owed

---

[10] R. Henchion, *The Graveyard Inscriptions of the Cathedral Cemetery of Cloyne, Co. Cork*, (Midleton, 2001), p. 163–4.

[11] Cork City and County Archives, U681 52/17/26.

[12] Registry of Deeds, Book 217, p. 70, no. 142395.

[13] Registry of Deeds, Book 234, p. 348, no. 153549.

[14] Registry of Deeds, Book 292, p. 583, no. 193338, Book 307, p. 589, no. 206167.

Shannon £30 a year for the head lease.[15] Apparently this and the running costs of the house were still too much for William Lumley. Within a few years his in-laws the Forsters took over his sub-lease.

For a short time, the Forsters and Lumleys shared Ballymaloe House; Mary's elderly parents both died there. But soon the Lumleys moved out and Mary's brother moved in. To formalise the position, in 1782 Abraham Forster took a lease from Longfield for 160 years which like the head lease between Shannon and Longfield was renewable forever. William and Mary Lumley moved to Ballycrenane, further down the coast towards Ballymacoda, with their son Hugh, while their other son William moved to Cork and went into business.[16] It was better to be in the city; Ballymaloe was too far out. Cork businessmen all owned property but once they moved out to a country mansion their fortunes declined and they soon floundered. Cork was a thriving port in the eighteenth century but to take advantage of that you had to be in the city where deals were done, positions were filled and ships were loaded.

Young William Lumley married Elizabeth Perrier, daughter of a Huguenot family from Brittany, whose brother Sir Anthony was a jovial and successful businessman. Knighted and twice invited to meet the king, Sir Anthony gave a merry account of these interviews and how King George had invited him for dinner. Sir Anthony was mayor of Cork, an agent for assurance and pioneered a new distilling technique which was not really successful. Young William and Elizabeth lived at Douglas House which was outside the city but near the docks at Passage West. Lumley and Sadlier were sheriffs of Cork in 1785 and William was director of the public coal yard and had moved into the city by the time of his death in 1818. His only daughter married her cousin William Lumley Perrier. Meanwhile his brother Hugh moved to Youghal and was there in the 1820s, sometimes described as a merchant, sometimes as a gentleman.[17]

There were still Lumleys in Cork in the twentieth century. Lumley and Co. specialised in equipment for the wine and spirits trade: racking, lifts and pumps, wine bins, brewers' requisites, aerated water and so forth. Their time at Ballymaloe had been short, less than two generations, but the eighteenth century

---

[15] Registry of Deeds, Book 354, p. 133, no. 236964.

[16] Registry of Deeds, Book 402, p. 485, no. 265448.

[17] Cork City and County Archives, SM 50/1, No. 21; B. Burke, *A Genealogical and Heraldic Dictionary of the Landed Gentry of Great Britain and Ireland* (London, 1858), p. 1,184; *Cork Constitution*, 21 Dec, 1826, Election, voters list; J. Fairbairn, *Fairbairn's Book of Crests of the Families of Great Britain and Ireland* (Baltimore, MD, 1993); National Archives UK, CSO/RP/1818/75.

saw the rise and fall of many fortunes. They had certainly left their mark on the structure of the house.

Mr Abraham Forster

The Forsters came to Ballymaloe just as the last great Georgian boom was picking up momentum. At first sharing the house with their in-laws, Mary Lumley's brother Abraham then became the pater familias at Ballymaloe. The Forsters, unlike the Corkers or Lumleys, had been in Ireland for centuries. The name is interchangeable with Foster and men with both names were prominent in the Pale and parliament. There had been Forsters in Munster in medieval times but they only moved to east Cork in the eighteenth century. A Thomas Forster had been agent to the Boyles early in the century but had been sacked for adding 'fictitious sums' to the accounts.[18] By mid-century Clement Forster owned property in Imokilly, lived in Cloyne and had a connection with Robert Longfield. The pattern of families attaching themselves to larger proprietors, acting as their agents and then emerging as substantial landowners themselves seems to be at work. Abraham Forster was made collector of excise at Cork while Richard Longfield was governor, which means that Forster was now attached to the Longfield interest.[19]

Abraham married into another leading Cork merchant family. His first wife Charlotte was the daughter of Sir Samuel Rowland – who was prominent on the common council – and after Charlotte's death, Abraham married her cousin Catherine Rowland. Charlotte and Abraham were married at St Finnbarre's in Cork in 1785 and the sum of £2,000 mentioned in the newspaper seems to be her dowry, which was certainly handsome.[20]

Cork was booming, for both Catholics and Protestants. Exports left Cork bound for every continent, while supplying the army and navy was a growing industry. When Abraham and Charlotte married, Britain was between wars, trade was expanding and Abraham was tax collector in the port and at its official heart. It was a complex job. Goods were taxed under several different headings, and with so much traffic, checking cargoes, filling in returns and enforcing collection took a strong character. Most Cork trade went to Britain; a Westcomb Forster was sending tallow to Bristol in 1789, but other cargoes went to the Caribbean, North America and Europe. The French Revolution had a great impact. It

---

[18] T.C. Barnard, *A New Anatomy of Ireland* (New Haven, CT, 2003), p. 229.

[19] For Lord Longueville's career, see Johnston-Liik, *History of the Irish Parliament,* vol. V, pp. 117–121.

[20] NLI, R. Folliott, *Biographical Notices in Newspapers Cork and Kerry, 1756–1827* (Index).

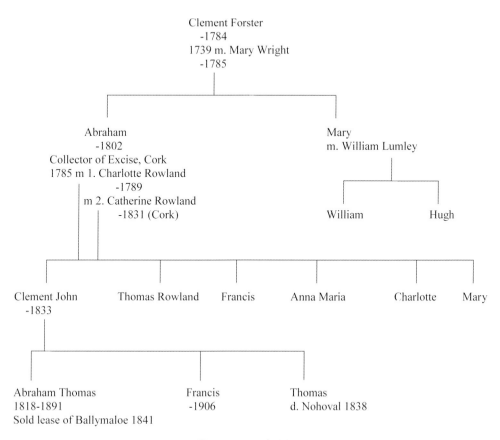

Forster Family Tree.

inspired revolutionary fervour and when rebellion broke out in 1798, Cloyne felt the effect. By then Longfield had become Lord Longueville and was at Castle Mary holding firm for government, but it was nasty enough; Longueville let Dublin Castle know that he had seen to the hanging of ten men. The revolution also precipitated two decades of war and the increased naval activity created the wealth of many Cork families.[21]

When Abraham Forster wrote his last will in 1802, he had a solid fortune to bequeath to his widow and six children, but the world in which he left them was much changed since the Act of Union. His two landlords, Lords Shannon and Longueville, had transferred to the parliament in London, which made it harder for them to control the local patronage and hand out plum jobs.

---

[21] J. Hayter-Hames, *Arthur O'Connor: United Irishman* (Cork, 2001), p. 184; Cork City and County Archives, U15B/B/2; National Archives, Ireland, 620/4/38.

Abraham wanted to be buried with his first wife Charlotte in Cloyne cathedral but left his second wife an annuity of £200 a year, 'three of the best horses I possess' and the use of 'whatsoever part of my household furniture, silver plate and china she may chuse', but to keep the whole intact for his son to inherit later, an inventory was to be made and signed by his widow. She could stay at Ballymaloe for a year until she found somewhere of her own to live.

Abraham had three sons and three daughters. The younger boys were left property in Cork, the girls were given money to be paid when they married. Abraham left annuities to his sister Mary Lumley 'for her separate use without the control or intermeddling of her husband' – a receipt in her own hand was to be taken for this money to make sure that she got it herself; Abraham had little time for his brother-in-law William Lumley. His principal heir was his son Clement John who was still a minor when his father died. He was to have Ballymaloe, Kilcolman and Kilboy in west Cork and Rathcoursey on the harbour, with several houses in Cork city and whatever personal fortune was left after the bequests. His landed property of course had to bear the cost of the various annuities.[22]

It seemed a fine fortune and on the strength of it Clement John completed the modernisation of the house which Hugh Lumley had begun. The large new structure which Lumley had created had shifted the whole plan of the building. Forster now altered the Jacobean core to create the fine Georgian reception rooms and staircase which are central to the current house. The front wall and the roof over it were left intact but the openings were altered. The chimneys too remained untouched but a new staircase was built between the two reception rooms which were of equal size to give the house symmetry. Behind the staircase was a window looking north, a classic feature of Georgian architecture. The rooms had new Georgian fireplaces set into the original hearths and the upper part of the chimneys was rebuilt in brick. Brick gave smooth or level surfaces, which was attractive to builders now that detailing was becoming more sophisticated. Plaster decoration was added to the reception rooms. The openings in the front wall were reshaped to create a pure façade with long windows and a wide door; all giving the maximum interior light. With this renovation, the main entrance to Ballymaloe House returned once more to the south. The enclosed yard to the east, still a stable yard with a coach-house, also developed as a service area for tradesmen and servants with steps leading down to the valley floor where the pantries and wine cellar were situated.

Despite these changes with their suggestion of abundant wealth, there was another family resident at Ballymaloe throughout much of this period. The fashion for directories and surveys brought travel writers to Ireland; William

---

[22] National Archives UK, PROB 11/1398/169.

Wilson's *Post-Chaise Companion* of 1784 listed 'Ballymaloe, the improved seat of William Abbot Esq. and anciently a very remarkable place'. Leet's directory thirty years later told the same story, but in Pigot's of 1824 Ballymaloe Castle was 'the seat of CJ Forster' and Samuel Lewis in 1837 called Ballymaloe the 'property of Mr Forster'. Either the Forsters sub-let it for about thirty years or both gentlemen resided there, one using the wing.

Communications had improved, bringing passengers and mail into the area from Dublin and elsewhere. The Dublin mail coach went through Fermoy once a day and took twenty-five hours to reach Cork while the Waterford to Cork coach went through Tallow, by-passing Imokilly. But both Youghal and Midleton were post towns, so a short-distance mail coach clattered along the road through Castlemartyr frequently. They were important to the economy and questions were asked in the House of Commons about the routes they took and whether mail could be speeded up.[23]

Typhus was a scourge in the nineteenth century and fever hospitals were being built to treat it. When a charity ball was held in Midleton under the patronage of the Marchioness of Thomond, Clement John Forster was on the committee. The aim was to add a fever ward to the 'Dispensary' of the town.[24]

Clement married Margaret Cuthbert of Garrettstown near Kinsale. They had three sons who would live in more difficult times than their father. The end of the Napoleonic Wars caused a collapse of Cork trade; not long afterwards the banks failed and many merchants lost their business. Clement had inherited a good property portfolio and when he died in 1834 he passed it on to his three sons. The eldest, Abraham Thomas, had Ballymaloe and Kilboy; the second, Francis, had a house on Sidney Place, Cork, on the ridge to the north of the city, 'with the lands thereunto attached'. Francis inherited the property on North Main Street, Cork, which included part of the Beamish and Crawford distillery site with adjoining houses; this was a sound investment as brewers generally do well during a recession. The remaining lands at Rathduff and Kilcolman were shared between them.[25] At the end of the century Francis put up a memorial inside Cloyne cathedral for his parents. A Michael Forster 'late of Ballymaloe' had been buried at Kilcredan churchyard out towards Ballymacoda in 1818.

The middle son Francis joined the army, became a lieutenant in the 4th Dragoons and later became a colonel. At Ballymaloe the family's position was deteriorating. The farm was divided; 46 acres were farmed by Thomas Lawless, a good friend of Clement John's, while part was held by the Longfields. Richard,

---

[23] *Parliamentary Papers, 1780–1849*, vol. 9, p. 133 for May 1842.

[24] *Southern Reporter and Cork Commercial Courier*, 4 Sept. 1841.

[25] National Archives UK, PROB 11/1830.

Lord Longueville, had died many years before and the head lease now belonged
to Rev. Robert Longfield of Castle Mary. He let £50 worth of Ballymaloe land to
his son Mountifort, presumably to qualify him as an elector, but when Mountifort
inherited Castle Mary in 1841 he gave this up.[26] In the meantime the Rowlands,
who were cousins and executors of the Forsters, had moved into Ballymaloe.

Not long after Clement's death, his youngest son was killed in a local tragedy.
The paddle steamer *Killarney* left Penrose Quay in Cork on 19 January 1838 in
a bitter easterly wind, with fifty passengers on board, and several hundred pigs.
When it came out into the wide bowl of Cork harbour it was clearly not making
much headway, which the passengers thought was the result of having so many
pigs on board. They put out to sea but turned back as the weather was so rough.
There were severe gales that month which caused havoc with shipping in the
Irish Sea. The *Killarney* anchored in Cove harbour for some hours, unable to
tackle the heavy seas outside the harbour mouth. However, the captain decided
to continue and they steamed out of the harbour, by which time it was late and
many people had gone to their cabins. At two in the morning, shouting warned
everyone to come up from below as the ship was swiftly taking on water. Baron
Spolasco, a medical man who was one of the passengers, reported that it was
washing through his cabin from the water closet as the sea was coming up
the outflows. He hurried on deck as the ship rolled and heaved but the mist
obscured even parts of the ship. Many of the pigs had been washed overboard.
Despite every effort at the pumps, the *Killarney* could not hold her course and
was wrecked not far off the harbour mouth at Novohal to the west. Many of the
passengers were drowned but survivors clung to a pinnacle of rock for two days in
appalling conditions awaiting rescue. The locals were said to be more interested
in salvaging the pigs. Baron Spolasco had already befriended Thomas Forster,
'a young gentleman of pleasing and unassuming manners'. Slowly the survivors
perished, 'poor Forster fell from the rock head foremost who, if not already dead
from starvation was nearly so'. Mr Collis, also struggling, exclaimed and 'poor
Forster is gone! I heard his neck crack' but the waves instantly carried him off.
It had in fact been Forster's suggestion to try to get into Robert's Cove but the
weather was cruel and, once wrecked, Forster could not survive the conditions.
'This was one of the most melancholy deaths that occurred among us,' said the
baron, who survived to write his account.[27]

The Longfields had the head lease of Ballymaloe and the owner was still the
Earl of Shannon of Castlemartyr, a Whig politician who sat in parliament in
London, but a pattern had emerged among the tenants. Successful businessmen

---

[26] *Parliamentary Papers*, (1836), vol. 43, p. 6.

[27] B. Spolasco, *Narrative of the Wreck of the Killarney* (Cork, 1838).

from Cork took the lease and moved to Ballymaloe where they did extensive new building, but within three generations the family ran out of money and sold on the lease. Now the pattern repeated.

Cork had fewer commercial advantages in the nineteenth century; the great boom years had ended, so Abraham Thomas Forster was lucky to find a buyer for the lease. He renewed it with Longfield in 1841 and then assigned it to John Litchfield the following year.[28]

The Rowlands moved out and when they did, they took with them the two paintings which belonged with the house – of Chuffe and the jester – which they hung in their new home at Ballinacurra.

Abraham Thomas Forster moved to the Kinsale area, where he lived as proprietor of Garrettstown, which belonged to his young cousins whose guardian he was. His brother settled not far away. Once more carts came to the yard at Ballymaloe where furniture and furnishings were loaded up, trunks lifted up onto the flat bed of the vehicle and horses led into the shafts. With a jingle and clatter one family left and another moved in.

---

[28] Registry of Deeds, 1842, Book 8, no. 76.

CHAPTER TWELVE

Mr Litchfield, Gentleman Farmer

In 1841, Ballymaloe was a very substantial house with gracious reception rooms, a pretty Queen Anne wing, two floors of bedrooms, stables and farmyard with a kitchen garden and plantations. John Litchfield moved to Ballymaloe a few years before he signed the lease, a common arrangement so that prospective tenants could try out the house and see if they liked it. Clearly it pleased John for he took on the lease at a rent of £285 a year. He was a bachelor when he moved to Ballymaloe, but his two spinster aunts lived there for part of the time, their other home being at 17 Patrick Street in Cork. John's father William lived in a fine merchant's house on Factory Hill above Glanmire which he rented from the Hoare family who had started the first bank in Cork. The origins of the Litchfields' wealth however had been created in the city during the boom days of the previous century.[1]

The Litchfields had been in Cork throughout the eighteenth century and done well. John Litchfield was listed as a silk merchant in 1787, then as a linen draper and by 1810 his firm had expanded into a second premises and was also selling furniture. It had been a magnificent trading century and the wealth created from land speculation and then sea trade had spawned fine merchants' houses around the city as well as country mansions of great beauty. All of these had to be furnished with the latest fabrics while the owners and their families could afford splendid clothes. At first trading in Cork city at North Main Street, then opening a warehouse in South Mall as well, it was John Litchfield the elder who at the beginning of the nineteenth century really cemented the family fortune. Like his contemporaries he invested in property; one or two were fee farm grants but most were long leases which could be sub-let for profit. This was the pattern; merchants who had built up capital invested in land and moved away from the city to a country seat. A fee farm grant was similar to a modern freehold but hard

---

[1] Registry of Deeds, 1842, Book 8, no. 76; *Guy's Cork Almanac*, 1844.

to come by; the terms of leases varied enormously. Eventually this system crashed – like the child's game of pass the parcel, the music stopped and a single owner had to be identified.

John Litchfield the elder lived in Cork city and married Ann Spiller, who brought a generous dowry. They had ten children, who were young when their father died in 1805. The father set up a trust fund for them and appointed as trustee Sir Samuel Rowland, who was a leader on the Cork Common Council and a cousin of the Forsters. Litchfield's two eldest children were his principal heirs but it was one of the younger boys, William, who prospered sufficiently to rent a merchant prince's house at Glanmire. It was he who took up the lease of Ballymaloe but it was his son John who went to live there.

John was the only member of his family to go to Trinity College, Dublin but his main interest seems to have been farming. Previous owners had had farming enterprises as well as other occupations: John Litchfield ran a farm and lived as a country gentleman. Throughout his life he was found at stock auctions or taking prize animals to shows.

He had hardly taken over the castle and lands of Ballymaloe when the potato crop failed. John Litchfield was on the Kilmahon Relief Committee but it was an alarming and distressing time with fever clinics set up in every village and crowds of angry poor at the gates of Castlemartyr or ransacking bread shops in Cloyne.

Nonetheless, John's aged aunts who lived in Patrick Street, Cork, also spent some part of the year at Ballymaloe. They were bookish and genteel, subscribers to Tuckey's *Cork Remembrancer* and *A Spiritual Commentary on the Book of Genesis* when those titles were published. Aunt Albina died at Ballymaloe in 1849, the year of John's marriage.

John Litchfield's wedding was held at Killeagh and his bride was Sarah Hewson, the daughter of the late Rev. Maurice FitzGerald Hewson who had been rector of Clonpriest near Youghal where the family lived. Sarah's brothers were in the Church too and one of them had married John's sister Charlotte. Sarah's father had died two years earlier when her brother had taken over the living of Clonpriest. Sarah's family came from Kerry and they had the Knight of Kerry in their family tree, which gave Sarah a claim to gentility which was important to her. When they married, John was thirty-two and Sarah eighteen. They started a family immediately – William was born the following year. When John's father died, the Litchfields gave up the house on Factory Hill and John's mother came to Ballymaloe, where she died in 1857.

It was a Victorian household of genteel manners and some discomfort. The reception rooms were large and although log fires could warm them it took many loads of timber. There was no running water in the house. The food however was good; local meat, fish from Ballycotton and vegetables from the fine walled garden below the house. The kitchen was in the wing with a range for cooking.

John's life was typical of a country gentleman of his day. He was a justice of the peace and sat on the Cloyne bench. On the Famine Relief Committee and the Dispensary Committee and concerning himself with agricultural breeding and the issues of small farmers, he was paternalistic and attentive. His swine were shown at the Royal Agricultural Improvement Society. He wrote to the landlords' solicitor on behalf of four small farmers who needed to clean their streams but were prevented by a neighbour. 'I know the river wants cleaning badly and suppose it is some crossness on the part of Smiddy that prevents him obliging the others.' He wrote again for John Cotter who would be late coming in to pay his rent, as 'he is wanting for my thrashing machine, and it is my fault his not having it before this'.[2]

Like his grandfather, he could fuss. There was a bad-tempered exchange of letters with Mr Keane of Shanagarry House about a supposed anonymous letter 'purporting to reflect on the Cloyne bench of magistrates' about which 'I beg leave to say that the statements contained in that letter are utterly untrue'. Litchfield absolutely denied that the magistrates had been whispering to each other. Mr Keane wrote crossly to the *Cork Examiner* in reply, expostulated that his letter had in no way been anonymous as everyone knew it was from him, and he named many witnesses who had seen the whispering. Someone, he said, was sitting as magistrate who was not supposed to be there.[3] And so local life rolled on.

Sarah's dowry was partially invested in government stock and partially in land near Castlemartyr. John had a portfolio of property, with over 800 acres on various forms of tenure, with tenants on most of it. He farmed about 200 acres at Ballymaloe throughout his life but he also had land near Castlemartyr and the Commons of Cloyne which he generally let. Much land was encumbered with mortgages and marriage portions; there was a nervous moment when the mortgage on one of his properties seemed likely to be charged against him, but luckily his cousins' trust fund had to pay.[4]

The Litchfields had six children, three boys and three girls: William, Caroline, Maurice, Helen Maria, Jane and John, known as Jack. By the time they had left the nursery for the schoolroom and the eldest, William, was almost grown up, the family's affairs were in disarray. Farming and rental incomes had not risen, but the costs of Ballymaloe and the family were mounting. The Provincial Bank of Ireland got a judgement against John Litchfield, who 'does not follow any trade or profession but is a gentleman', for £5,100.[5] At the same time the

---

[2]   Cork City and County Archives, U229/119/3; U229/85/6.

[3]   *Cork Examiner*, 24 Aug. 1867, 27 Aug. 1867.

[4]   Registry of Deeds, 1853, Book 29, no. 22.

[5]   Registry of Deeds, 1867, Book 29, no. 67.

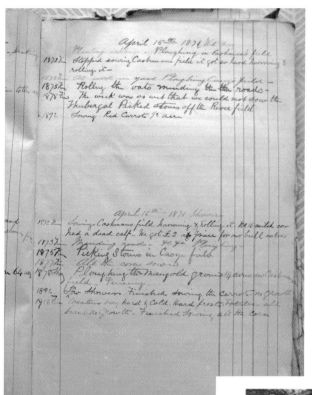

49. *William Litchfield's farming diary, April.*

By kind permission of Rory Allen.

50. *Wilson Strangman.*

© Newton School, Waterford.

CARAGH LAKE 'CAMP' – SUMMER 1957
Wilson Strangman

51.   Ballymaloe House in the early twentieth century.

52.   Muriel and Terence McSwiney with their daughter.

Photograph, Cork Public Museum.

53.   *Captain Jim Simpson.*

54.   *Jim and Helen Simpson,*
at her wedding to Tom Morgan,
Midleton, spring 1952.

55. Helen Simpson in the Litchfield veil.

56. Wedding group, Helen Simpson to Tom Morgan, 1952.
Front row R to L: Joan, Helen, Tom, Priscilla.
Back row: Jim, Hugh de Costobadie, Marion Simpson, John and Valerie Dring,
unknown, Muriel Morgan, unknown, unknown.

JOHN CONDON & SON'S AUCTIONS

BALLYMALOE, CLOYNE, CO. CORK

Attractive Auction of this beautiful old Geraldine Country Seat and Castle, with the Residence, Well-Stocked Gardens, Pleasure Grounds, Gate Lodges, and a large quantity of valuable Hardwood and Conifer Timber, standing in 403a. 1r. 19p. of excellent quality (mainly Limestone) Land, with extensive range of Outoffices.

The Property, which is situate in the fertile Barony of Imokilly, two miles from Cloyne, six miles from Midleton and nineteen miles from Cork, in the United Hunt country, is **eminently suited for a Stud Farm or Training Ground**, and possesses a great name for the excellence and quality of the Stock raised on it. Low Revised Terminable Annuity, payable to the Irish Land Commission: £96 1s. 6d. Provisional Poor Law Valuation; Land £366 15s.; Buildings £67 5s.

JOHN CONDON & SON have been instructed by Captain J. M. Simpson (acting on the medical advice to lessen his activities) to sell the above Property by Public Auction at the Imperial Hotel Pembroke Street, Cork, at the hour of 2 o'clock p.m. (S.T.) on **Thursday, October 16th, 1947.** Vendor reserves the right to sub-divide should this course be considered desirable to suit the requirements of intending purchasers.

Should the Property be sold in Two Lots, the divisions will be:—

LOT ONE.—Ballymaloe Demesne, containing 217a. 2r. 39p. with the Residence, Castle and Gardens, subject to the Revised Terminable Annuity of £68/8/8.

LOT TWO.—The lands of Ballyduff adjoining Lot One, containing 185a. 2r. 20p. subject to the Revised Terminable Annuity of £27/12/10.

The Farming Stock, Implements and Miscellaneous Effects will be sold on the Property at a later date. Descriptive Pamphlets are now ready and will be forwarded on application.

Further particulars and cards to view may be obtained from:—
MESSRS. BARRY M. O'MEARA & CO., Solicitors, 18 South Mall, Cork (Tel. 189) or from
JOHN CONDON & SON, M.I.A.A., Auctioneers and Valuers, Youghal, Co. Cork (Est. 1869). (Tel. 25 Youghal)   4131

57.   Sale particulars for Ballymaloe, 1947.

58.   Ivan Allen with jersey herd.

59.   *Jersey herd on the avenue.*

60.   *Ivan Allen with the milking machine.*

61.   *The Allen family c. 1958. L to R: Rory, Wendy, Tash, Yas, Ivan, Myrtle, Tim.*

62.   Rory and Tim Allen on top of a car.

63.   The driveway as it was in the 1950s.

64.   The front façade in the 1950s with Ivan, Myrtle and friends.

65.   *The Allen family in 1977.*

66.   *Myrtle Allen cooking.*

67.   *Anne MacCarthy in the Yeats Room.*

68.   *Joe Cronin delivering the post.*

69. Joe and Rita Cronin in 1991.

70. The dessert trolley.

71.   *Ballymaloe House as night falls, 2015.*

Photograph Joleen Cronin.

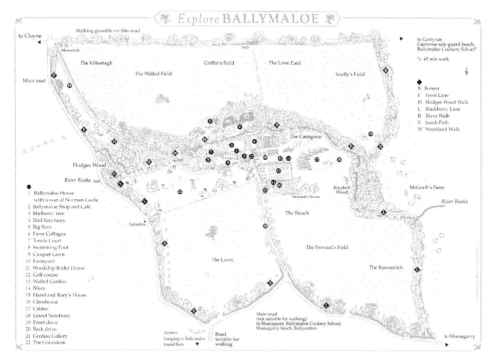

72.   *Explore Ballymaloe.*

Map © Marina Langer.

73.   Hazel Allen.

74.   Rory Allen on guitar in the hall.

75. *President Bill Clinton on stage in the Grainstore at the Worldwide Ireland Funds Conference in 2012.*

76. *President Bill Clinton with Mrs Allen.*

77. *The drawing room.*

78. *The dining room.*

79. *The courtyard.*

80. *The green drawing room.*

81. *The roof.*

82. *From the roof, 2015.*

83. *The swimming pool.*

84.   *The walled garden.*

85.   *The kitchen.*

86.   *The conservatory, long room and the new bedrooms.*

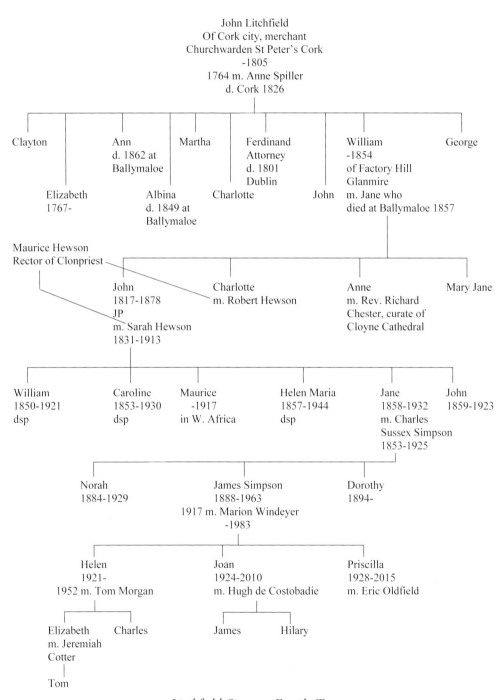

Litchfield-Simpson Family Tree.

government was passing legislation to untangle the web of entailed and indebted estates. Property sold through the Landed Estates Court was washed of its legal tangles and given clean title, debts were paid and the vendor got any balance. Under this arrangement John and Sarah Litchfield put three lots up for sale in the spring of 1870, but the remainder of their estate was also up for sale by regular auction. Included was Ballymaloe and Parkylessig, 193 acres with 'the castle or mansion house and out-offices' on a lease for 160 years dating from 1790.[6] Only one of their properties was in fee farm, all the rest were leases. The tenants were listed as solvent or on small leases and the income from letting was given in the advertisements.

The results of the sale were published in the paper the following week. Lot 4 – Ballymaloe – had not sold. The Litchfields had dismantled their property portfolio but still had Ballymaloe with rent to pay to the Longfields and the cost of keeping it up. Overseas markets had pushed down the price of grain and meat; it was a tough time to support a country mansion from farming, but they did have a few government stocks and had raised some cash from the sale.

John Litchfield died a few years later, aged only sixty-one. His son William had already taken over the management of the farm and worked hard at it. Perhaps this gradual descent from the comfortable rectory of her childhood to the genteel money worries of her widowhood marked Sarah and explained the attitudes of her daughters, or perhaps they simply reflected their times. It was a beautiful place to grow up; they had servants, employees on the farm, good food and a place in local society, but it was not comfortable, there were many anxieties and a declining income.

The children found it hard to make independent lives. Maurice somehow disgraced himself. He was sent to West Africa and in later years, if children asked about him the adults tightened their lips and said, 'We don't talk about him.' Jane was the only one to marry. She met an Englishman, Charles Simpson, who was a friend of the Penrose-Fitzgeralds who were then at Rostellan Castle.

Charles Sussex Simpson worked in London and his parents lived in Middlesex. Both Charles and his brother Marmaduke were underwriters at Lloyds of London. Charles and Jane became engaged and the wedding was arranged for 19 April 1881. The night before his wedding Charles stayed with the Penrose-Fitzgeralds as the service was at Cloyne cathedral. Jane's uncle took the service.

The Simpsons returned to England and settled at Little Melton in Norfolk. They had three children, a boy James and two daughters Dorothy and Norah. Jane often brought her family to Ireland and Charles, who had a camera, took a few photographs of Ballymaloe.

---

6   *Cork Daily Southern Reporter*, 31 Mar. 1870, 2 Apr. 1870.

Jane's sisters and brothers never married. Caroline became engaged and a house was bought from Mountifort Longfield of Castle Mary on a mortgage in 1886. But something was discovered about the prospective bridegroom, the family decided he was unacceptable and Caroline's marriage was called off.[7]

There had been another attempt to sell Ballymaloe; it was put on the market in May 1883 but withdrawn for lack of bidders. 240 acres were included in the sale, of which all but four were farmed by the Litchfields. This is probably the same holding that Simon le Blund had inherited centuries before. The executors of Patrick Wise were petitioners in the sale but once more Ballymaloe did not sell.[8]

After Jane's marriage and their father's death, the household settled to a pattern. William was head of the household but his widowed mother Sarah had authority. William ran the farm and was an attentive and conscientious farmer. He kept a diary in which the heading was the date and the entries were by year so that he could compare the activities of the day with those of previous years. Horses were vital for the fieldwork and there are many references to them. There were twelve dairy cows and a herd of sheep but much of the farm was arable. William grew barley, oats and wheat as well as field vegetables – potatoes of course, turnips and mangolds, but also crops of beans, carrots and cabbage. In 1892 he bought a Hornsby combined mower and reaper for £14. The summer months were taken up with harvesting hay and then corn, during the winter months the livestock were brought in which meant feeding and yardwork. William sowed winter wheat in November and began ploughing in January. By March he was manuring his potatoes.

Caroline and Maria Helen, known as Myra, lived a life of late Victorian gentility, with tennis at the Midleton Lawn Tennis Club, tea parties with the neighbouring gentry, occasional guests to dinner or drives out to visit country houses nearby. Jack was given a job working for his brother-in-law in London but while Charles Simpson was away from the office, Jack insured an unseaworthy Greek ship against the guidelines of his brother-in-law. The ship was scuttled and Charles lost a great deal of money. Jack lost his job and returned to Ballymaloe where he liked to shoot and had a fondness for drink but few useful skills.

They never tried to sell the house again. Instead they took on neighbouring land – at Ballymaloe Begg from the now very indebted descendants of William Penn and at Ballyduff to the south. It was all good land and farm prices began to improve once more. In all, William Litchfield farmed 604 acres. All the same there were borrowings; William paid off a mortgage in 1910 not long before further taxes fell on the estate.[9]

---

[7] Registry of Deeds, 1886, Book 5, no. 57.
[8] Sale particulars, 1883.
[9] William Litchfield's farming diary, private collection.

For short journeys, the Litchfields used a jaunting car which was a light vehicle drawn by one horse and ideal for trips to neighbours or into Cloyne.

Their friends lived nearby, the Rowlands at Sleiveen were very close and Hewson cousins used to visit. The Litchfields were sociable and had a network of friends among the local gentry. The Strangmans in Shanagarry were also nearby; Thomas and Sarah Strangman were a little younger than Sarah Litchfield but the families knew each other well. The Strangmans had been brewers in Waterford until they married into the Pike family who were bankers. As the Pikes were Quakers, the Strangmans gave up their brewery out of respect for Quaker beliefs.[10] The family had been at Kinoith since about 1830. Thomas and Sarah Strangman had three children: Lydia, Wilson and John Robert. They often visited Ballymaloe, which was then decorated in late Victorian style, the hallways rather dark and crimson fabrics creating a pleasant ambience in the dining room. The colours were deep and warm, but the house was very cold.

One of the sons, Wilson Strangman, later wrote memoirs about this period:

> At the end of the nineteenth century, Ballymaloe started being At Home on Friday afternoons during the winter months. I was old enough now to recognise, in some degree, the distinctiveness of Ballymaloe's atmosphere. William and Jack had been no further than to Midleton College. Caroline, Myra and Janie had all, I think, been educated at home. Yet Ballymaloe had a quiet and unperturbed assurance in social contacts that might well have been the outcome of much wider experience in youth. Ballymaloe entertained with an unconscious friendliness and ease. This unassuming friendliness, though accepting and expecting the social limitations of those times, pervaded the whole atmosphere of its rooms. Everyone in the 'social' life of Cloyne met at Ballymaloe.[11]

The young men played ping-pong in the dining room and when it was time to go home, they made their way through the back kitchen with its flagstones and guttering candles, then out into the stable yard to look for their coachmen. The Ballymaloe coachman had a house in the yard, beside the coach-house and stables.

> In the gusty darkness of the night some of us would gather around the coach house door in the Ballymaloe stable yard to summon respective cars. There were three outstanding coachmen who, probably, had been enjoying the At

---

[10] E. O'Kelly, *The Old Private Banks and Bankers in Munster* (Cork, 1959), pp. 23, 27, 36–9.

[11] W. Strangman, *Memoirs*, unpublished in private collection.

Home in their own way. There was Larry Litchfield, a stout, heavy, slow-moving man whose real name was Neill: there was Mick from Kilcrone, Sir Warren Crooke-Lawless's coachman and there was Regan. Larry and Regan loved to spar; they both thoroughly enjoyed it. The wit and repartee of those two was always amusing and sometimes inimitable.

With the gusty night about us, with the smoky gleam of a carriage lamp fitfully playing on half discernible forms, with the ring of horses' hooves on the cobblestones, and with a square of diffused candle light framed by the back kitchen's door, I can hear my brother's voice in the darkness saying: 'Oh Larry, I've forgotten to congratulate you.' Then Larry's slow cautious reply, cautious and curiously soft in tone. Yet somehow impregnated with a sense of enjoyment in the coming tussle.

'Why so, sir?'

'I heard you got first prize at Midleton Show for the fattest coachman.'

'Oh but sir, he's …' Regan's voice would break in, and then the two of them wold be at it. My brother had merely started them off.

Then Minnie Gabbett's conveyance – whatever it was I've forgotten – would move off through the night for the front door.[12]

Wilson Strangman described the rooms as shabby and spacious, 'with their old china and their old silver and sometimes their carpetless floors'. But he felt it did not matter, that the old china looked just as well and the Anglo-Irish chatter was just as merry and unconcerned.

They climbed into their carriages. 'The mare would not stand, she had had enough of Ballymaloe; she was fidgety and restless, dancing to be off on the road and away home.'

Although life had this charming continuity, radical changes were already underway. Land ownership was altering; laws had been passed ever since the Famine. Renewable leases had been converted in favour of tenants, so the Longfields duly improved their lease on Ballymaloe with Lord Shannon.[13] Complex titles had been simplified so that land could be sold. Land acts gave tenants the right to buy and the funds to do so; gradually large estates were dismantled. The system was creaking; Lord Shannon mortgaged his Castlemartyr estate including Ballymaloe in 1883 and with each land act, the days of the Irish landlord system dwindled.[14]

Wilson Strangman describes how: 'Shortly before my brother sailed for South

---

[12] Ibid.

[13] Registry of Deeds, 1902, no. 204.

[14] Registry of Deeds, 1884, Book 1, no. 206.

Africa, Ballymaloe gave us a small dinner of farewell.'[15] John Robert died in Orange River County in 1908.

> It was shortly after my father's death [in 1907]. My mother was too much of an invalid to get about. Ballymaloe's guests were only my sister, my brother and myself. Old Mrs Litchfield sat at the foot of the table – was it the head? William at the other end. I sat beside Mrs Litchfield with my back to the fire; my brother was on the other side of the table but not directly opposite me. Where Caroline, Myra, my sister and Jack sat I don't remember.
>
> We had roast chicken for dinner. Logic whispers in my ear that old Mrs Litchfield would have been too frail and blind to have carved, yet I have a definite and decided feeling that carve she did! I can see the delicate round of the fragile eyelids on the old, old eyeballs and the frail hands fumbling with the carving knife and fork as the spent tissue and bone gripped the handles.
>
> Personally I have no fault to find with the Ballymaloe dining-room of those days. I liked its dark red walls; a sense of dusky richness; a suspicion of it is not out of place, to my mind, in a room of its size. The light of the lamp, soft, warm and not very powerful, fell on the table, on old Mrs Litchfield's white cap, on her pale skin and on her eyelids stretching now rather markedly over the curve of her eyes, and then lost itself in the shadows and the old silver of the room.
>
> Towards the end of dinner my brother stood up and proposed Mrs Litchfield's health, a little decoration that came quietly and easily to him. Thus youth pledged age though the sands were running low for both of them.[16]

Sarah Litchfield died in 1913. By then the family owned Ballymaloe Castle with its 240 acres outright. Untangling the leases was complex but under the Land Acts, the Litchfields bought Ballymaloe. In 1906, William Litchfield recorded in his diary 'Signed agreement for purchase of Ballymaloe.' That meant a new debt; the Land Acts provided funding for tenant purchase which had to be paid back so much a year. There were also death duties, as Sarah and her children all had a share in the family inheritance. By some complexity of title, in 1912 Caroline Litchfield owned Ballymaloe in fee simple but the following year 'in consideration of natural love and affection' the ownership had been transferred

---

15 W. Strangman, *Memoirs.*

16 Strangman, *Memoirs.*

to William. He died soon afterwards, in 1921, and left it equally between his siblings, who all paid another round of inheritance tax.[17]

Caroline was the eldest of the daughters, a sweet-natured woman, artistic but very deaf. Myra was the youngest but far more assertive. Caroline painted landscapes in watercolour and had a small studio at the back of the house. She attended Mr Skully's classes in Cork where she befriended Muriel Murphy, daughter of the Cork brewing family. Unlike the Litchfields, the Murphys were Catholics. They were well-off and Muriel had had a genteel upbringing, educated largely at home. By the time she met Caroline Litchfield, Muriel had been strongly influenced by the growing movement for Irish independence. She used to come to stay at Ballymaloe and painted a picture of the old castle. Towards the end of the First World War as pressure mounted for Irish freedom, Muriel caused a sensation. She told her family that she was going to stay at Ballymaloe with her friend Caroline Litchfield but instead she slipped away to England to join her lover. Terence MacSwiney was leader of Sinn Féin in Cork and had been interned following the Easter Rising. He had been deported to England and held at Bromyard in Herefordshire where Muriel was able to join him and marry him. MacSwiney had planned not to marry because his life would be too hard for a wife but Muriel was a beauty and genuinely fired by both independence and the emerging labour movement. Terence MacSwiney told his sister, 'The girl I was coming to love so intensely could match my mind.' Terence and Muriel married in June 1917 and had a daughter, Máire, but they had little time together. MacSwiney was rearrested in 1920 while lord mayor of Cork and died in Brixton prison after a hunger strike lasting seventy-four days. When he died Muriel collapsed and could not go to the funeral. She never came to Ballymaloe again. At first she was prominent in the Irish freedom movement but she subsequently left Ireland, and lived first in Germany, then in France. She remained a political activist all her life but lost custody of her daughter to Terence MacSwiney's sister. Muriel died in 1982.[18]

Terence MacSwiney's funeral cortege in both London and Cork displayed the depth of feeling building up over Irish independence. Violence increased, leading to war. Castle Mary was set on fire and gutted. The Penrose-Fitzgeralds left in

---

[17] E. Brennan, *Landlord and Tenant Law* (Dublin, 2010); The explanation for Caroline Litchfield's title to Ballymaloe may be the mortgage at the time of her cancelled marriage: Registry of Deeds, 1884, Book 34, no. 195 and 1886, Book 35, no. 57. Caroline's title is Registry of Deeds, 12 April 1912, no. 280, the transfer to William in Litchfield records, private collection.

[18] M. MacSwiney, *Dictionary of Irish Biography* (Cambridge, 2009).

1921 – 'never to return', their neighbour wrote sadly.[19] At Ballymaloe, Jack lost his rifles when the IRA raided the house and stole his two Purdeys, which infuriated Jack who prized them highly. But Caroline managed the alarming situation with unexpected calm. She had her mother's fine engagement ring in a drawer of the dressing table in her bedroom but while the men were going through the house, Caroline went coolly up to her room. One man told her to 'come back out of that' but another said, 'Leave her alone, she's deaf and half daft.' The men were behind her as Caroline moved over to the dressing table and tucked something inside her bodice. In fact, she had saved the engagement ring and the next week's wages for the men. By acting the fool Caroline got away with it. Unlike many others, the house survived. The Simpsons heard that their two maids were the sisters of one of the local IRA men, Davey Walsh, and the girls used to feed the IRA men, so when there was a dinner party at the house, the freedom fighters ate well. Whether this connection influenced events, or the fact that Ballymaloe was not the seat of a landlord, the house escaped the fate of many Cork houses and was not burned.

William Litchfield died in 1921, the year before the Irish Free State was created and the Civil War which followed. Jack kept the farm going as best he could, but he had often been ill and he too died in 1923. By then the war was over. Jack recorded only two entries in the farming diary:

> 1922 August 13th, Republican Army defeated in Cork.
> 1922 August 14th, Men hiding in lofts from Free State Army.[20]

The two sisters, Caroline and Myra, now in their sixties, were left with a large mansion, no menfolk and a farming business. The Civil War was over but the country was still unsettled. What were the two Litchfield ladies to do?

They turned to their nephew in England. Their sister Jane and her husband Charles had three children, one of them a boy named James. Jane had brought her children to Ballymaloe regularly for holidays with her family, so they knew the old house and in turn they were known in the area.

The boy James Simpson had been born in 1888 and trained as an engineer. He was in his twenties when the Great War broke out and he joined the Norfolk Yeomanry, but because of his engineering skills he was transferred to the Royal Army Service Corps where he became a captain. During the war, he had met a young Australian girl, Marion Windeyer, who was a nurse in London, serving in the Voluntary Aid Detachment. Theirs was a wartime romance and wedding;

---

19   Cork City and County Archives, Bennett Diary, B609/9/A/41.
20   William Litchfield's farming diary, private collection.

they were married in London in 1917. By the early twenties they were living in Norfolk where James had an engineering job, and they had a daughter Helen. The aunts in Ireland called on Jim to come over. They needed someone to run Ballymaloe and in any case, he was their natural heir. So they offered him a position as manager, with the in-built proviso that he would one day have Ballymaloe himself.

Jim Simpson agreed to come. He and Marion packed their trunks and set off for Wales with their baby daughter, to take the steamship to Cork and make a new life at Ballymaloe.

CHAPTER THIRTEEN

Captain Simpson and His Family

When the Simpsons came to Ballymaloe in 1923 it was still a Victorian household. The drive led directly to a gravel sweep outside the front door which was protected from the weather by a porch with windows in it. The antlers were in the hall, the furnishings were patterned. The bedrooms were cold and damp; the top floor was used as garrets. Although light came into the gracious rooms from the long windows, at night they were shadowy as candles struggled in the large spaces. It was Victorian too because the Litchfield sisters lived and thought as their parents had taught them despite the great upheavals of the early twentieth century in Ireland.

Captain Simpson thought it his duty to take on the place and help his elderly aunts, but it was difficult for both him and his wife. Caroline and Myra Litchfield saw themselves as high in the social scale of east Cork but they had had little education and no opportunity to broaden their outlook. To them, Marion Simpson was a colonial; poor Jim had made an unfortunate marriage and they made the young wife feel that.[1]

Marion's background and outlook could not have been more different. She came from a distinguished Australian family. Her grandfather Sir Charles Windeyer was a judge and attorney-general in Australia and an honorary doctor of laws at the University of Cambridge. Marion's mother was active in charity work and women's suffrage, her father was a barrister, her great-aunt was among the first female graduates in New Zealand and Marion had a degree from Sydney University. Keen on education and women's rights, the Windeyers were far removed from the values of Caroline and Myra Litchfield. Marion had grown up in Sydney and nursed in England; her experience was a world wider than that of the Litchfield aunts.

---

[1] Much of the material for this chapter has been taken from conversations with Helen Morgan and Priscilla Oldfield.

The aunts treated Marion as a social inferior and often wounded her to tears. Jim was paid £30 a year as manager, while the aunts owned the business and wrote the cheques. They were cautious and meticulous, as they probably needed to be, but if Ballymaloe was to survive it needed energy and commitment. Jim had these but he often had to drive improvements through against elderly resistance.

The farm was a mixed one, with cattle, sheep and crops. Jim continued with his uncles' system of mixed farming but made some changes. There was a milking herd of dairy shorthorns with a milking parlour at the bottom of the farmyard. The sheep grazed the pastures and lambed in spring. Jim grew barley for malting and oats but did not grow wheat. Beet and mangles were field crops and the market gardening enterprise was an important part of the farm. Jim kept seven horses for field work but he also crossed them with better animals to breed jumpers.

Fourteen men worked outdoors, three of whom were in the garden. Two women worked in the house, a cook and a house-parlourmaid, both of whom wore black-and-white uniforms. The aunts used the drawing room and the Simpsons the small sitting room at the back of the house to the north. Beyond the dining room was a small pantry with a locked store cupboard and beyond that three steps led down to the stone hall. The kitchen was in the wing, but beside the stone hall were various small rooms used for household chores. Cooking was done on the range and the kitchen had no plumbing – just a cold tap outside the door – but it had good windows from which you could look down the drive and see visitors arrive. Aunt Myra had rooms upstairs in the wing where the kitchen range created some warmth.

The house was very cold. Log fires used up enormous amounts of wood but still could not warm the large rooms in the dead of winter. Jim Simpson had no control over the cheque book but gradually he made basic improvements. The nursery was on the first floor over the dining room with the night nursery beside it. As a trained engineer, Jim tackled innovations himself. He made a stove for the nursery by bending a sheet of metal; the flue went up the chimney and the nursery became the only warm room in the house. Rain water was collected and there was a good spring. Jim put a tank in the north-east corner of the roof-space and fixed up a pump to fill it. Then he put in a lavatory and a bathroom. The aunts were shocked at that. Larry Neill the coachman had brought up large jugs of water from the kitchen every morning and they had always used a hip bath on two blankets. 'Surely,' the aunts said wrinkling their noses, 'you're not going to take all your clothes off.'

Jim and Marion's eldest daughter Helen was two when the Simpsons moved to Ballymaloe. When Marion got pregnant again the aunts were quite horrified to think of what the young Simpsons had been doing in their house. Yet when two more girls were born, Joan and then Priscilla, they became very fond of the

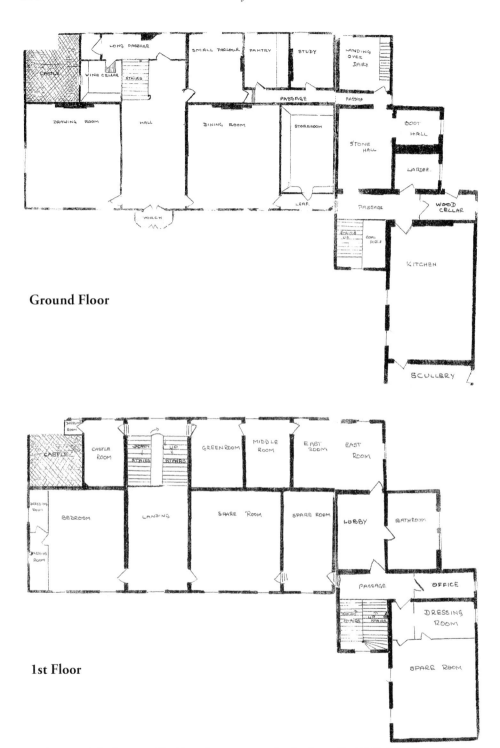

Ground Floor

1st Floor

Plan 5. The layout of Ballymaloe 1923–1947, by Priscilla Oldfield. Not to Scale.

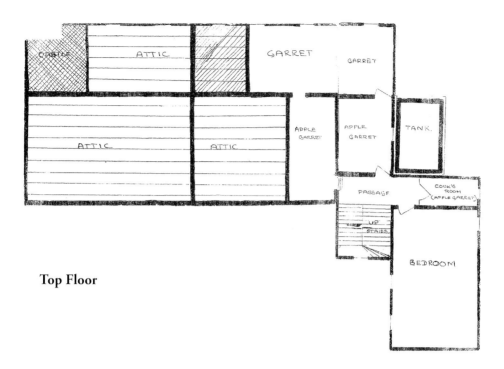

Top Floor

children. Caroline in particular used to have them on her knee and tell them stories about a shepherd and his dog Rover.

Jim and Marion had to fit themselves into this old-fashioned household with the genteel strictures of the aunts, the discomforts and limited income. It was very frustrating for Marion, who was university educated, to live with two old ladies whose ideas were so limited and who treated her badly. The little girls felt this tension but were fond of their elderly aunts. They loved the farm and later remembered with affection the people who had worked on it.

Dan Doolin, whose father Jim had worked at Ballymaloe, was steward and lived in the house to the south-east of the walled garden. Morris Veal lived in one of the gate lodges and his daughter Molly became nursemaid to the children – 'I loved her dearly,' said Helen. Ned Veal was also there as carpenter. The Griffin family have been at Ballymaloe for several generations: Eddie worked on the farm, his father had been head gardener and his granddaughters Breda and Susie are still there in 2016. Every week John Ridney the blacksmith came out from Cloyne to attend to the seven working horses.

Jim Simpson had previously been offered a job in Morris cars as he had known Morris at university, but Ballymaloe took priority over any other career. So he used his engineering skills to modernise farming methods and installed an engine underneath the floor of the grainstore with a long shaft which could be used to drive various tools. This shaft ran the milking machine, the grinder, two crushes, a saw, a blade for 'fingering' turnips and another for slicing them. As soon as he could, he got a car; the little girls rushed down to see the Citroen when it first arrived. But driving to Cork was a tiresome journey. Jim came back one day glowing because he had got there and back without having a puncture – usually the broken surface and stones meant getting out and mending a tyre, perhaps more than once on the way. Tractors only came later, in the 1930s. The working horses were draft mares but Jim Simpson put them to blood stallions in order to breed jumpers bought by the Irish army or the jumping team. The mares had to be sent away but the aunts were perplexed by that. As a child, Helen never heard them use the words ram or bull – they referred to 'the animal'. When the mares went to the stallion, they discussed how odd it was that the lady horses went on holiday when the men horses did not. The Simpsons were partly amused and partly infuriated with this obtuse gentility.

The Strangmans had been friends of the house for many years but Wilson and Lydia were the same age as Jim and Marion Simpson, so they became very close; the Strangmans used to walk over every Christmas Day for tea. Although the house seemed old-fashioned to the Simpsons, there was a billiard room over the hall, a tennis court and bicycles. The grounds had changed from the pleasure gardens of the Georgian design; at the back of the house was thick laurel so the children never saw old Sir John FitzGerald's carved stone.

Jim had a radio receiver, also part of his engineering skills. In their small sitting room at the back of the house, which was warmer than the drawing room where the aunts sat, he and Marion could listen to the broadcasts. When the maids brought tea though, the Simpsons noted that they had milk in their jug whereas the aunts had cream.

The aunts reminisced about the past and spoke of their mother as 'dear mama'. They had very definite ideas about behaviour and standards that had to be kept up, 'as long as there's a Litchfield alive …'. Caroline was a sweeter character than her sister. She was very deaf but a good artist, with her small studio at the back beside the pantry. She died long before her sister, in 1930. She had been staying with the Strangmans at Kinoith in Shanagarry but one morning she never woke up. Brought back to Ballymaloe, she was laid out in her coffin, which stood in the hall before burial in Cloyne cathedral. Priscilla, the youngest child, known as Pillie, was a toddler. She was discovered rattling the handles of the coffin in the morning, calling, 'Aunt Cally, Aunt Cally, come out of that.'

Caroline had made a handwritten will witnessed by two maids. Aunt Myra had to sign a declaration that it was genuine because the document was so informal. The witnesses, Margaret and Nellie Walsh, could not be consulted as one had died and the other had emigrated to America. The will was very simple: Caroline left £300 to each of her nieces – Jane's daughters – and everything else to Myra.

The Litchfields had some investments, most of which were British government bonds, which gave a modest income. This will too created an inheritance tax bill.[2]

Aunt Myra, who was younger than Caroline and who lived much longer, became a solitary figure in the household but was still the owner and controller of the cheque book. She belonged to another time. John Bennett of Ballinacurra, who owned the malting business there, noted in his diary for 29 May 1930, 'Having drawn a blank at Castle Mary I hiked on to Ballymaloe and found the Simpson family at tea with my old friend Myra Simpson the last survivor of the old generation reminding one of the younger years and tennis days in the 90s of the last century when as yet I had not become obsessed with yacht racing or able to participate for lack of cash and of ability to leave home.'

Bennett was then in his sixties, a little younger than Myra. He kept diaries all his life and his entries give an idea of the social world in which the Litchfields had lived. Bennett recounts visits to Castle Mary, which was rebuilt in the 1920s, and tennis parties with the Rowlands at Ballinacurra House. He shot at Fota with Dorothy Bell and her husband Billie, where Hugh French and Andy Rowland were among the other guns.

The centre of this little circle of Protestant gentry was the cathedral in Cloyne. They went for matins every Sunday, made communion there and held their christenings, weddings and funerals in the enclosed choir of the old building, since the nave was far too large for their small congregations. This was the world in which Caroline and Myra had spent their lives.

The Simpsons were introduced to this circle but made friends of their own in the area, the closest of whom were the Strangmans at Shanagarry. Wilson Strangman was a bachelor who lived with his spinster sister Lydia. Wilson was a gentle, rather feminine, man, and very kind to the Simpsons – the little girls adored him. They loved Lydia too, who they knew as Lil. Helen thought her 'one of the nicest women I ever met'.

The Strangmans, whose background was in commerce and banking rather than land, were well-off. Lydia later paid for the Simpson girls' schooling. At first Helen was sent to a boarding school in Dublin 'which was unbelievably holy. If you were bad, you were put on a dais and prayed for.' She was very unhappy and soon transferred to Newtown, the Quaker school in Waterford.

Wilson Strangman was a governor and benefactor of the school. He paid for several children to go there and had many of the pupils to stay both at Kinoith and at his lodge in Kerry where the children could swim and go boating. During the first term that Helen was at Newtown Ivan Allen, who had been at the school himself and had stayed with the Strangmans before, was involved in a car accident

---

[2] National Archives of Ireland, Will of Caroline Litchfield, 1930, date of grant 13 August.

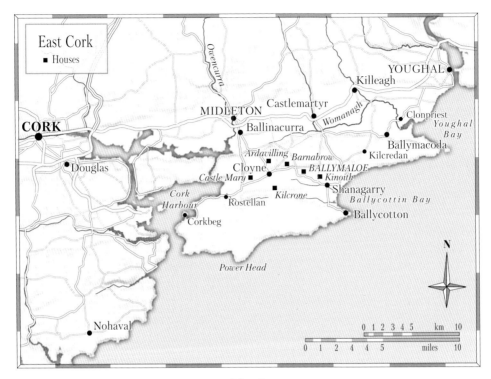

Map 8.

and came to convalesce at Kinoith. His friendship with the Strangmans was to be a lasting one. He came to work for Wilson as manager and became his farming partner. Wilson Strangman had a substantial farm at Shanagarry which included a horticultural business, with orchards and a market gardening enterprise. He grew violets which were sent to market in London; children had to bunch them up for sale. Jim Simpson saw that flowers might be a profitable venture and grew daffodils at Ballymaloe which he sent to Friday market in Cork. Horticulture was rewarding and Jim came to love the Munster Autumn Show to which he took his fine Cox's apples.

The Simpsons had other friends: Mrs Coxwell-Rogers at Kilcrone who dressed like a man and had a daughter called Fay who was gentle and feminine like her name, and the Stackpoles who lived at Ardavilling. Charles Creed of Cloyne House trained racehorses which he sometimes brought over to gallop at Ballymaloe. He took Jim to the races in Dublin. The Merediths at Barnabrow had daughters the same age as the Litchfield girls. It was Dick Meredith who showed Jim how to make the girls' nursery stove.

Jim's mother Jane came back to Ballymaloe as a widow. When Charles Simpson died, Jane and her daughter Dorothy, known as Didge, moved into Ballymaloe

Cottage and stayed there until Jane's death. Dorothy was then free to return to Norfolk where she spent the rest of her life. Norah Simpson died very young of cancer.

The drive to the Ballycotton gate was lined with elm trees which later died from Dutch elm disease. Across the road from Ballymaloe was a shop and forge, near the current Ballymaloe Cottage. This was all part of the Litchfield property then, but was let. A wheelwright worked at the forge, which was useful to Jim Simpson. Jim became treasurer of the Ballycotton lifeboat, which became an important part of his life; he was often down in Ballycotton.

Marion made all the children's clothes, knitting socks, jumpers and warm knickers. It was a wonderful life for the girls. As they grew older they could go off in the fields, taking a few slices of bread and spending the summer days outdoors. Sometimes they would be taken to the beach. In warm weather, they could climb up on the roof, take off all their clothes and sunbathe since no-one could see them.

The girls might have been happy, but for the Simpsons and for Marion in particular, life at Ballymaloe was often a strain. Aunt Myra never softened towards Marion and often made her cry. Jim would leave the house when his aunt was especially awkward and go to see the cattle in Ballyduff. As long as Myra was head of the household Marion's role was very limited, but after Myra's death 'she turned into a really gifted gardener'.

For Jim and Marion, keeping Ballymaloe solvent was always a worry. There had been death duties to pay after John and Sarah's deaths, then William, Jack and Caroline's. The loan for the freehold purchase also had to be paid off. Although wages were low, the cost of keeping the place up was high compared to farm income. When she grew older, Helen moved into the castle room. When she asked one day if she could light a fire as her shoes were growing mould, Jim told her to bring them downstairs and brush them off.

The Simpsons sold butter; some of it was even sent over to the Longfields in London. It was Helen who often made the finished pats and wrapped them in paper. The men separated the milk, turning it in a large hand-over-hand churn before tipping it out into a long wooden trough. Then the solids had to be cleaned and made into even pats of butter, wrapped up in waxed paper ready for market. The cellars, which Helen called 'the caves' because they were built into the rock, were always cool and perfect for storing the dairy produce. With Wilson Strangman's help, Jim built a large greenhouse in the field below the walled garden where he grew tomatoes to send into Cork. Every enterprise helped to raise the total farm income.

Gradually some improvements were made. Clothes and sheets were boiled in an old copper tub in a place outside the kitchen known as the Bleach, and the laundry was hung on strings in the kitchen to dry. Jim put in an Aga with a water tank so the kitchen got hot water, though the tank had to be filled by hand every day. But on the farm, de Valera's Ireland posed new restrictions. During the economic war, farmers could only buy Irish livestock. The dairy shorthorns and large white pigs bred in Ireland were all they were allowed and were often of poor quality, which used to infuriate the farmers.

The only telephone was in Ballycotton, where the postmaster Bob Marley had one. There was no electricity; it reached Cloyne after the Second World War.

The Simpsons and Strangmans had been close friends for some time. When Ivan Allen came to work with Wilson Strangman, he too befriended the Simpsons. Although Ivan was a generation younger than Jim, they lived nearby and both were enterprising farmers.

Helen, Joan and Priscilla had friends from school, from the local area and in Cork. There were parties now at Ballymaloe for the young people. When Joan had a party on her sixteenth birthday, her school friend Myrtle Hill came, whose grandfather and father were both architects in Cork. Ivan Allen was at the party, where he met Myrtle for the first time.

Aunt Myra was now in her eighties. Priscilla remembers her as a 'funny little white-haired woman with black and grey clothes'. She had been cruel to their mother but, all the same, 'I think we were very fond of Aunt Myra – we called her Aunt Dodie.'

The Simpson girls were very pretty, Helen the tallest of the three, Joan and Priscilla more petite. They were just growing up when war broke out. Helen worked as a nurse before going to university at Trinity where she had a bad fall which damaged her coccyx and necessitated many operations. Joan joined the Women's Royal Air Force. Myrtle Hill too went away to do war work, but a romance blossomed and she married Ivan Allen in 1943 when she was nineteen. They moved into the Red House, near to the Shanagarry farm and Ivan's work with Wilson Strangman. Priscilla, who was younger and grew up after the war, went to work in the office of Harry Hill, Myrtle's father, but then moved to London where she studied architecture at night school and worked at an architectural firm called Bennett's.

The war interrupted trade and created shortages. At Ballymaloe fuel became a problem. They got in a stock of anthracite but only dared light the range on Saturday night to have a good lunch on Sunday. Through the week, one of the maids used an old-fashioned cauldron in one of the outhouses to make stews.

Aunt Myra died in 1944 at the age of eighty-seven. Apart from small personal gifts, Jim Simpson was her sole heir.[3] Once more there were death duties; Jim Simpson paid them five times in twenty-five years but at least he now had full

---

[3]   National Archives of Ireland, Will of Maria Helena Litchfield, 1944, File No. 9768.

control of Ballymaloe. He sold 150 acres with Ballymaloe Cottage to pay the death duties and other borrowings. But Ballymaloe was not his for very long. By 1947 he found it impossible to keep it going and decided to put it up for sale. Helen was sad; as the eldest she had often been told that she would inherit it, but her father 'was put to the pin of his collar to keep it going'.

John Condon and Son of Youghal were engaged to auction Ballymaloe. The sale was held at the Imperial Hotel in Cork on 16 October 1947. On the day of the sale, Ivan Allen drove Jim Simpson up to the city. There was a keen interest in the land among local farmers and many came to the sale out of sympathy with the Simpsons. Ivan and Myrtle attended the sale to give the Simpsons support. However, a period of economic nationalism had weakened the Irish economy and finance was scarce. No-one had come to bid and Ballymaloe did not sell.

Wilson Strangman and Ivan Allen were by then partners in Imokilly Orchards, which owned the house at Kinoith and the Shanagarry farm, with the horticultural business which they had built up there. Wilson Strangman knew the difficulties of Jim and Marion Simpson's situation. Equally, Ivan and Myrtle Allen were keen to try new ventures. To Wilson Strangman, a purchase by Imokilly Orchards would help everyone. The Simpsons would make a good sale and be free of the property, while the Allens could expand the farming business and take on the old house while they were young and willing to tackle it. An offer of £12,000 was made for Ballymaloe and accepted.

The Simpsons bought a house in Midleton and left the old castle. When they moved out they took with them the green marble fireplace from the drawing room which Jim adored and which he installed in their new home.

The three Simpson girls married. Helen's husband was Tom Morgan, a barrister who later turned to farming, and they settled at Carrigaline. Joan married Hugh de Costabadie. Priscilla married an Englishman, Eric Oldfield, and settled in Hertfordshire. Jim and Marion Simpson stayed in Midleton where Jim died in 1963 and Marion in 1983.

Ballymaloe was sold to the Allens in 1947 but it was another two years before they took up residence. Ivan took the farm in hand at once but the house was altogether another proposition.

CHAPTER FOURTEEN

The Allens of Ballymaloe

As soon as the Allens bought Ballymaloe, Ivan Allen began to farm it. He increased the size of each enterprise, rented more land and poured his considerable energy into farming and horticulture. It was unusual for a farm to have a young couple as owners, especially such an enterprising pair as Myrtle and Ivan. For two decades Imokilly Orchards, based in Shanagarry and including the Ballymaloe land, was the largest employer in the area – until the restaurant eclipsed farming as the main activity.

Ivan was not born into farming but came from Drogheda to attend Newtown, the Quaker boarding school in Waterford which had a strong reputation. Wilson Strangman had a remote property on Caragh Lake in Kerry where he took schoolboys to swim, fish and go boating and Ivan had been on these expeditions. He had also stayed at Kinoith, so when he left school Wilson asked Ivan to help manage his farm. In 1932 Ivan, aged seventeen, came to Shanagarry and went into horticulture. Wilson sent him to England to research apple varieties and orchard methods but Ivan also learned about tomato growing and came back with fresh ideas on horticulture, which were put into practice at Shanagarry.

Once he bought Ballymaloe in 1947, Ivan started farming on a much larger scale. He doubled the size of Jim Simpson's herd to ninety cows and bought Jerseys for their high butter-fat milk which went to the creamery in Mogeely. From here the whey came back to feed a herd of pigs. Like Jim Simpson, Ivan came up against animal restrictions; breeds from England or elsewhere were banned even if the Irish breeds were less productive. Ivan managed to bring some landrace pigs in from Northern Ireland which did very well, until an outbreak of swine fever meant the whole herd had to be slaughtered.

When Ivan and Mytle Allen took possession of the property, there was a sense that Ballymaloe House might not survive. Captain Simpson had done his best but the house was cold and uncomfortable; when he took the marble fireplace from the drawing room, the gash in the hearth seemed to symbolise the decrepit state of Ballymaloe. The house had been modernised very little, and in any case many of its kind did not survive; some were burned, some became neglected, while others were demolished when farmers took off the roofs to avoid paying rates. Land was precious but country mansions were not. Famous Irish houses like Bowen's Court sank into piles of stone and there was perhaps a danger in 1947 that Ballymaloe might be going that way. Instead, the house acquired dynamic young owners who brought it back to life.

Ivan and Myrtle Allen had met Philip Pearce whose family had a printing business and bookshop in London. During the war Philip had moved to Ireland as a conscientious objector and had married Lucy Crocker, a nutritionist and teacher who came from London to join him. Philip's design skills and Lucy's ideas on health chimed with the forward-looking attitude of the young Allens. They became friends and Philip built a house for his family called the White House on one of Ivan's fields in Shanagarry. The Pearces went back to London at the end of the war but did not stay there long as their eldest son Stephen suffered from the smog. When the Allens decided to buy Ballymaloe, Philip borrowed money from his father in order to become Ivan's partner in the farming business there.

While Ivan expanded the farming, Ballymaloe House was renovated in ways that Jim Simpson had never been able to tackle. The Allens engaged Ken Bayes as architect and undertook a large restoration project on the house. New bathrooms and lavatories were put in and a kitchen created in the alcove, the small room beside the dining room. The porch was taken off to leave wide double doors of wood. The top of the staircase was remodelled, which altered the shape of the hall. Before this, there was no passage at the back of the house, so the bedrooms opened one into the next. By enlarging the ceiling of the hall, there was space for a landing which opened into a new passage. The house was wired for electricity which was now available under the rural electrification scheme and heating was put in, while the walls of the large reception rooms were dry-lined to protect them from damp.

Finally in 1949 the Allens moved in; bright lights came on in the rooms at night and shone out onto the gravel sweep. Myrtle and Ivan had modern tastes and bought furniture with simple lines. Soon after moving in, they made their first visit to Denmark to learn from Danish farming methods. This trip also influenced their ideas on design; they picked up some of the modern Scandinavian ideas on style and returned to Denmark in 1955. Most of all, their country offered opportunities. A republic had recently been declared by the government of Ireland and a new state was growing with a young generation to shape it. Ivan and Myrtle Allen were a key part of that generation; they had modern tastes and ideas. They brought up their children with the Quaker ethos, industrious and fair-minded, but this was mixed with a liberalism which was supportive and free-spirited, having thrown off the Victorian past. Post-war

Ireland was a mixture too; of a freedom-loving republic and a suffocating conservatism with deep nostalgia for a lost past. Ivan and Myrtle carved their own style among those influences.

They already had two children when they moved to Ballymaloe, while four more were born in the house; Wendy, Natasha, Timothy, Rory, Yasmin and Fern all grew up there. Myrtle spent a great deal of time feeding them all and as Ivan was a discerning eater she collected recipe books and paid close attention to ingredients. They were all around her, in the garden, on the farm with fresh fish close by at Ballycotton.

Myrtle had been born in Cork city, in Tivoli and grew up at Monkstown on the shore of Cork harbour. Her father Henry Houghton Hill and her grandfather Arthur were architects; Henry had designed many of the buildings which went up in Cork after it was burned during the War of Independence.[1] He and his wife Elsie had two daughters, neither of whom went into architecture and Henry died in 1951 so never saw the great success which his younger daughter Myrtle made in another professional field.

Changes to the house had left the wing as a separate structure with a kitchen already in place. When Philip and Lucy Pearce came back to Ireland with their three children, they moved into the wing. Lucy had been a teacher in London but as a social reformer she had been part of the Peckham Project which tried to improve the health and well-being of working-class children by exercise, natural food and better communication. Lucy had well-developed ideas about food and cooking. Philip had hoped for a role in Ivan's farming business but as a designer and printer, farming did not suit him. Instead he began to make pots in the old greenhouse where Jim Simpson had grown tomatoes. Fascinated by pottery he went to Cornwall for a year to learn his craft. Clear that this was what he wanted, he made a deal with Ivan. The old Glebe House in Kilmahon was part of the Shanagarry property owned by Imokilly Orchards, so they did a swap; the Pearces became owners of Kilmahon in exchange for Philip's investment in the farm business at Ballymaloe.[2] Once there, Shanagarry Pottery grew into a successful business which helped define the style of Irish crafts from the 1960s. The period when both families lived at Ballymaloe had allowed a tremendous cross-fertilisation of ideas.

Both the Pearces and the Allens were close friends of Pat Scott, the artist, whose work Ivan admired and collected. Ivan began to build up a collection of Irish art, including work by Jack Yeats.

---

[1] *Dictionary of Irish Architects 1720–1940,* www.dia.ie, entries for Hill, Henry Houghton and Hill, Arthur.

[2] Kilmahon Glebe is part of Shangarry South on Griffiths Valuation 1845 and subsequently.

After the Pearces left Ballymaloe, the wing was advertised for holiday lets in the English papers. Families began to arrive for their summer holidays and many of them are still visiting. Ballymaloe has a warmth and attraction that never fades; people keep coming back.

As Richard Wood, a family friend writes, 'There was a special atmosphere at Ballymaloe, one which was carefree, friendly, and tension-free, indeed peaceful, though not in the silent, dull sense but rather alive – and harmoniously alive.'[3]

Meanwhile Ivan's farming enterprise grew in size and output. Joe Cronin came looking for work in 1951 when jobs in the area were scarce. As he says now, 'they never told me to leave so I'm still here.' He was part of the workforce of twenty-five men at Ballymaloe while another hundred people worked at Shanagarry. By enlarging the business, machinery became cost-effective and at one time Imokilly Orchards had ten tractors. Ivan rented more land: at Barnabrow, at Clonmult near Dungourney, 'Smyths' or Ballyonane, Ballybranock and Geoghans, the last three all near Cloyne. At one time Ivan had a joint enterprise with Harry Roberts at Ballyanna on the coast. Besides the dairy herd and pigs there were beef cattle and a flock of 300 breeding sheep. They grew a variety of crops; barley but not for malting in deference to Quaker temperance traditions, and oats but not wheat. Root crops were important; early potatoes, sugar beet and onions, but they also grew field vegetables like cauliflowers. At Shanagarry there were glasshouses where mushrooms and tomatoes were grown. Some were sold in Cork, but the main market for mushrooms was in the UK.

There was a railway station at Mogeely then. Mushrooms were picked early to catch the mid-day train from Mogeely to Cork, where they were loaded onto the Inisfallen, the ferry which sailed to Wales. They were called Rooskah Valley Mushrooms and each chip basket had the name of a town in Wales or England marked on it, so that they could be dropped off at the correct stations.

Ivan and Myrtle were not just farming but helping to set up the organisations which were so essential for education and marketing – the Co-op, the marts and Macra na Feirme – the young farmers club. Hurrying to Shanagarry in the morning to manage the large workforce there and keep the orchard work on schedule, Ivan would also have to keep the other holdings running efficiently before he and Myrtle rushed away to a meeting of one of the growing organisations they helped to create.

Myrtle Allen stood for president of Macra na Feirme in 1959 but a priest objected to her sending Irish boys to 'heathen foreign countries' where they might be open to dangerous influences. He went to every meeting and spoke against her, making her candidacy impossible. To Ivan and Myrtle agricultural

[3]   Richard Wood, '*Memoirs*', unpublished.

education and learning best practice wherever it might be found were essential for Irish farming.

Wilson Strangman was still at Kinoith but was now very elderly. His sister Lydia had died in 1949 but he outlived her by almost two decades. Myrtle's family came to Ballymaloe briefly. Her sister Moira married Colonel George Payne in India and when they returned they lived at Ballymaloe Cottage for about three years until they moved to England with their son Desmond. In 1951, Myrtle's father Henry Hill died and arrangements were made for his widow to come to Ballymaloe. A bungalow was designed by Pat Scott and built for Elsie Hill inside part of the old walled garden, but she only lived there for a short time as she died not long after her husband, in 1952.

However, other families came to Ballymaloe and were welcomed. The Bauers were German and had set off in a boat for South America but were shipwrecked off the coast of Waterford. Destitute and unable to go further, they were rescued by the local Quakers and came to Ballymaloe soon after the Allens bought it. Mr Bauer was an engineer, so very useful in Ivan Allen's business. After Mrs Hill's death, they moved into the new bungalow in the garden. Mr Bauer had a workshop at the corner of the stable buildings, beside the current Ballymaloe Shop. When he died, his widow and daughter moved to Rathcoursey.

Wilson Strangman died of cancer in 1966. His only brother had died young and his sister some time before, so he had no close relatives. Ivan had been his business partner for many years and was co-owner with Wilson of Imokilly Orchards. Ivan inherited Wilson Strangman's share of the business. At the time of Wilson' death, Imokilly Orchards owned 214 acres at Ballymaloe More, 176 acres at nearby Ballyduff and 175 acres in Shanagarry, which included Kinoith House, the Shanagarry farm with its garden and orchards, as well as bogland beside the coast.[4]

As the Allen children got older they went away to boarding school, to Newtown at Waterford and two of them to Millfield in England. By the 1960s Myrtle was beginning to find the house rather empty and wondering what she would do next. Ivan later liked to recount how Myrtle told him, 'I'd love to do a bit of cooking'. He said he was not going to buy a restaurant for her; if she wanted to cook for the public she would have to do it at home. So in 1964, she hired two girls to assist with the cooking and enlisted her family to help prepare the house. They cut trees and made tables, a new electric cooker was installed and they put an advertisement in their local paper, the *Cork Examiner*. 'Dine in a Historic Country House. Open Tuesday to Saturday. Booking essential. Phone Cloyne 16', it read. They would open five days a week and see how they got on. The

---

[4] National Archives of Ireland, Will of Wilson Strangman, grant 18 April 1972.

restaurant was named 'The Yeats Room' because Ivan had hung his Jack B. Yeats paintings in the dining room.

Interviewed later by a graduate student for a PhD thesis, Myrtle Allen remembered that pivotal moment when the advertisement was in the paper and the restaurant would open the following day.

> 'I remember driving down the front avenue and quite rightly I was aware of the fact that it was my last day of freedom when I could get in the car and go off anywhere I wanted to and I knew I'd be tied to routine after that, for the rest of my life, and I was right. I pottered down the drive and I met a car coming up and it stopped. The man looked out the window and he said 'Is this where the restaurant is?' and I was delighted with myself.'
>
> 'Yes,' I said.
>
> 'Oh,' he said, 'I'm from Woodford Bourne and I want to sell wine to you.'[5]

The local wine merchant already saw potential.

Starting a restaurant was a challenge and Myrtle called on her eldest daughter to help launch the new business. Wendy returned from Switzerland to manage the dining room while Myrtle oversaw the kitchen. They had a core staff of two but they had to get more help from time to time and the staff numbers soon grew.

Dining in an Irish country house was a novelty in 1960s Ireland. There were the few established hotels but a restaurant in a private house was an unusual idea and many wondered how it would work. However, Myrtle had a great interest in food, excellent ingredients to hand and very high standards. Everyone was appreciative and a few customers became regulars, but at first business was slow. Then two years after the restaurant opened the *Egon Ronay Guide* gave The Yeats Room a very good rating which was reported in *The Irish Times*, after which, in Myrtle's words, 'business exploded'. But at this stage, Myrtle was doing all the cooking with only one person to help her, so they took guests for dinner only, not lunch, and were only open five nights a week.

When the restaurant opened the older children were teenagers, but Yasmin was nine and Fern only two. Ivan and Myrtle were exceptionally busy and needed help with the children. The boys in particular were mischievous. When the restaurant was closed and Ivan and Myrtle were out at meetings, Joe Cronin would take them to Shanagarry to see films playing in the hall there. *A Hard Day's Night* was

---

[5] M. Mac Con Iomaire, Edited Interview with Myrtle Allen, Ballymaloe House, (7/5/2003), PhD at School of Culinary Arts and Food Technology, DIT.

a big attraction in Beatle days. When they got cars, the wide doors of the house were a temptation. 'They drove the cars in,' Joe recalls, 'Minis you see, they drove them right up to the foot of the stairs, two of them – through the big timber doors – like barn doors they were then.' Later, the front door was redesigned. The large timber doors were removed and a new glass one installed with a fanlight inserted over it. There is now a small space between the outer panelled doors and the inner glass one, but the outer door of Ballymaloe is seldom closed.

Joe Cronin, who had done every kind of farm work for Ivan – in horticulture, tillage and with the sheep – now came into the house to serve drinks and help with the restaurant. Minding the guests was easier than minding the sheep and Joe had a gift for hotel duties. He ran the bar and then was the front of house manager, becoming a well-known figure to guests; even in his eighties he comes in the morning to do the post and bring the newspapers. Anne McCarthy, known as Anne Mac, came as a waitress soon after the restaurant opened. With her bustling style she has been a stalwart of the business for over four decades. The farm had been a big employer, both for men on the farm and for women who picked mushrooms. However for women in particular, the restaurant at Ballymaloe now became an important source of work.

In the restaurant, legal issues forced the pace. 'The Yeats Room' could serve wine but nothing else, whereas if the Allens had bedrooms available they could get a dispensing licence and keep a full bar. So gradually bedrooms were done up, both in the house where the large rooms over the reception rooms were divided, and in the courtyard where the coach house and stables with their loft above were converted to make guest bedrooms. In 1967 Ballymaloe officially became a guest house, serving three meals a day and open for most of the year. In that year the Allens' eldest daughter Wendy married Jim Whelan, the first of the children to marry. In fact, Wendy had to write to one guest, Mrs Wilkinson of County Antrim, to say that they couldn't give her lunch on 17 April as that was her wedding day 'and the house is being taken over for the wedding reception. Would you possibly be able to leave by about 10.30 that morning, because, as you can imagine we will be in a complete state of chaos.' For all its success it was still very much a family home.

After the death of Mr Bauer, Jim and Wendy Whelan moved into the bungalow in the garden until they moved to a house of their own in Shanagarry.

Ivan became more and more interested in Irish arts and literature. He collected nineteenth and twentieth century Irish paintings and his interests widened into the other arts: music and the Irish literary tradition. He drew in musicians like Liam Clancy who would come to stay, sing to the guests but also recite Yeats' poems. Liam enjoyed the hospitality, splendid food and pints; he often had to be collected several days later. Pat Scott designed for the Allens; René Hague made wall hangings, Louis le Brocquy's drawings hung on the stairs. Ivan and Myrtle at last tracked down the paintings of Chuffe and the Jester which had been removed by the Rowlands. They belonged with the house and now returned to Ballymaloe. So did the Cloyne harp, or at least a replica of the original was cast in resin and brought back to the house to symbolise the reawakening at Ballymaloe of its old culture, one of hospitality and Irish artistry.

As the restaurant prospered, Myrtle's interest in local food and traditional Irish cooking deepened. Other young women came to learn from her. Darina O'Connell came to Ballymaloe in 1968 and became Myrtle's sous-chef. In 1970 Darina married Tim Allen, the eldest son who was running the Shanagarry farm, and the young couple settled in the house at Kinoith which was made over to Tim in 1982.

Fern was in London in the early 1980s and wrote home to ask for money to do a Cordon Bleu cookery course. The answer was 'no, come home and learn how to cook here'. So cookery lessons began at Ballymaloe. Myrtle put another advertisement in the *Cork Examiner* offering a ten week course. Seven students signed up and Fern returned from London to join them. The course was taught by Myrtle and Darina Allen, working on alternate days. After Darina went on a cookery course herself in Italy she realised the enormous potential of their situation in east Cork where local produce was of such high quality. So in 1983 Darina and her brother Rory O'Connell opened the Ballymaloe Cookery School at Kinoith which has won an international reputation. Darina presented nine series of her television progammes, 'Simply Delicious', and published a series of cookery books. Many Irishmen blessed her as their wives began to experiment and the quality of home cooking rose – until the men themselves joined the courses. The trained chefs who emerged from the cookery school in turn opened restaurants and the growing standards of cookery in Ireland owe a great deal to Ballymaloe. Myrtle used recipes from the Irish rural cookery of the past – which showed how delicious the tradition had been – but brought them up to the standards and tastes of the present. Darina also broadened the scope of Ballymaloe's repertoire by bringing in teachers from overseas and incorporating modern techniques.

The cookery was winning a growing reputation but the house had to be run as a hotel with all its complex demands. Hazel Lalor came as an assistant in 1970. She had been studying hotel management and had worked in Canada; she was not keen to come home. 'Most hotels in Ireland at that time were pretty dreary. I was on a train and I just happened to read an article in a magazine about Ballymaloe. I decided that's where I wanted to work.'[6] She was asked to start work on 26 December which she thought odd, and when she arrived she found it fairly

---

6   *Financial Times*, Life and Arts, 7 Sept. 2012, 'At your Service', by Nicholas Lander.

chaotic with only one telephone in the building, still in the hall where it had been before the house became a business and at some distance from the office where the bookings were made.

Hazel applied her energy and efficiency to the whole business of hotel management. At the time, Rory Allen, the younger son, was working with his father in the farming business in preparation for an eventual handover. Rory was sent to New Zealand to learn their dairying methods; he spent a term at Massey University before working on several farms to gain experience. After some procrastination, Hazel went out to join him. They spent a year together in New Zealand and then made their way home overland. They were married soon after their return to Ireland, in September 1974, and moved into the bungalow in the garden. Hazel worked alongside Myrtle running the business, which worked well as Myrtle had always concentrated on the restaurant whereas Hazel took on the larger logistical task of both hotel and dining room. She sharpened the focus of the business considerably, helping to win Ballymaloe a Michelin star in 1975.

Hazel was also instrumental in establishing the walled kitchen garden as a key part of Ballymaloe, providing the fresh vegetables, herbs and flowers which are so much the tradition in country houses. The hotel made that viable once more and the garden gives the hotel guests great pleasure as they wander through the summer flowers and the plots of well-tilled vegetables.

The Allens' eldest daughter Wendy started her own business soon after her marriage. The Ballymaloe Shop sells Irish designer crafts, cookery utensils and books, reflecting the family interest in style and quality. In 1999 Wendy also opened a café so that visitors could have a light meal or a coffee as they browsed. Yasmin started her own Ballymaloe Relish business in 1990 when her children were still young. It grew swiftly and moved into purpose-built premises on Little Island near Cork.

Fern and Myrtle also started a café in the Crawford Art Gallery in Cork. Myrtle's grandfather, the architect Arthur Hill, had designed much of the building, so for Myrtle and Fern there was an added resonance when they opened the Crawford Gallery Café in 1986. Fern ran the café for many years and built up its reputation.

As Myrtle got older the pressure of the restaurant became harder to sustain and in 1994 Darina's brother Rory O'Connell took over as head chef. As co-founder of the Cookery School with his sister, he shared Myrtle and Darina's approach to food. Rory and Darina often emphasise the use of local unadulterated ingredients, while Darina and Tim have increasingly used organic methods on their land at Shanagarry. Food, after all, is at the core of all lives and farming defines how we live on the land, so food production has become an issue arousing strong opinions and public interest. Myrtle Allen lived out her vision of fresh local food cooked perfectly; Darina and Rory continued her vision, frequently speaking about food production on television and in interviews, which has exerted a slow but powerful influence on Irish and European attitudes to food. Rory's ten years in the kitchen at Ballymaloe House brought new recipes and a new dynamic to the kitchen.

Rory Allen had been dedicated to the guitar since he was at school. As a farmer and young father he had limited time for music, but as his five children got older he had more time to practise and would often play for the guests in the evening, just casually in the hall or drawing room. Naturally he made friends among the local musicians in Ireland's lively folk music scene. Gradually this blossomed into something far more ambitious.

As a guest house, Ballymaloe was in demand and new rooms were added. In the 1980s five new bedrooms were constructed on the lower ground level with a conservatory and new dining room above them. Since then there have been regular improvements and expansion. Four more bedrooms were added in 1996 and a large new room constructed over them named the Long Room, used both for dining and for receptions. The old piggeries were removed in 2000 and a big farm shed replaced them. In 2005 Rory Allen converted part of the farmyard into apartments and the old silage store became a house named the Tower.

Ivan was behind most of the construction; in fact his wife would sometimes try to prevent further building but Ivan's energy and vision got the better of her caution. However, Ivan did not live to see the last of these developments. He had handed over the Ballymaloe farm to his second son Rory in 1974 and gave his attention to the hotel. He was often to be found sitting in the hall, delighted to chat to the guests or take them out on excursions. The family grew; first grandchildren and then great-grandchildren were in the house or running in the garden. With very little warning, Ivan passed away on 31 August 1998. A Quaker service was held on the paved forecourt of Ballymaloe in golden sunshine followed by a simple Quaker burial in Cork.

Rory Allen had established regular music sessions in the drawing room at Ballymaloe in the 1990s and then biannual music weeks. In 2007 he embarked on a larger project by converting the old grainstore in the farmyard into a theatre and reception hall. It was completed in 2009 in time for his daughter Roisín's wedding. Now it stages concerts, hosts weddings and is used for film shows, classes, conferences and receptions.

Ballymaloe has been a leader among country house hotels and has set a standard for Irish cookery ever since Myrtle first invited guests to dine in 1964. She was given an honorary doctorate from University College Cork in 2000 and has received numerous awards for food production and cookery.

Her children and grandchildren have started businesses of their own in the area, in food, joinery and gardening. Although all six of Ivan and Myrtle's children have a share in the hotel business, the Ballymaloe farm belongs to Rory and is farmed by him and his son Darren. The Ballymaloe Cookery School at Kinoith made Darina into a household name not only in Ireland but internationally. Not just the food she prepared and her ability to teach, but the style and generosity she maintained amid hectic demands, have earned her great affection from pupils and other chefs. Her daughter-in-law Rachel joined the business and has a television series of her own. She too has published cookery books and has brought new skills but equal warmth to the business.

The original ethos was a winner. 'Ballymaloe is not run by fashion but by quality,' Hazel Allen says.[7] Quaker industry and Irish creativity, a strong family and the best of Irish country produce have formed a web of businesses which have at their core Ballymaloe House and its matriarch Myrtle Allen.

Ballymaloe has lived out all the changes of Irish history and returned to an earlier pattern. It began as a Gaelic farm, became a Christian settlement and then a Norman castle; it was a Puritan mansion and the country seat of several prosperous merchants. Now at last, Ballymaloe has owner-occupiers with a highly successful business and a family farm. Far more than that, it has re-established the Irish country house tradition of warm hospitality, living arts and some of the finest food in Europe.

---

[7] *Financial Times Magazine*, 8/9 Sept. 2012.

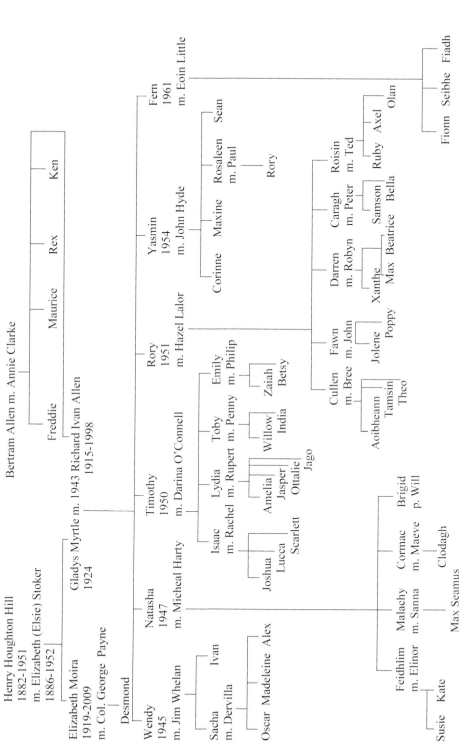

Allen Family Tree.

Allen pedigree dated 26 November 2017

m. married   p. partner

Appendices

Poems of St Colmán

Translated by Professor Donnchadh Ó Corráin

'Since he was a child in the cradle
the bright star
the name of the Man-Strength
surpassed every name.'

*   *   *

'I do not awaken to an improper poem
after a beautiful sweet-dreamed sleep
a Lentern command: to do nothing unpermitted
a drink [wine of the Mass] of requiems, the grace of the Royal Son.'

From: P. MacCotter, *Colmán of Cloyne: A Study* (Dublin, 2004), pp. 129, 131

The FitzGerald of Cloyne Harp 1621 – Inscriptions

(Translated from the Gaelic)

These are they who were servitors to John fitz Edmond Gerald,
at Cloyne, at the time that I was made, viz., the steward there
was James son of John; and Maurice.

Walsh was our superintendent; and Dermot son of John was
Wine Butler; and Shane Ruadhan was Beer Butler; and Philip son of
Donnell was cook there, in the year of our Lord 1621.

Teige O'Rourke was chamberlain there.

And James Russell was House-marshal; and Maurice son of Thomas,
and Maurice son of Edmond; these were all discreet attendants upon him.
Philip mac Teige MacCragh was Tailor there; Donough son of Teige
was his Carpenter, it was he that made me.

GillaPatrick MacCridan was my Musician and Harmonist, and if I
could have found a better, him should I have, and Dermot MacCridan along
with him, two highly accomplished men, whom I had to care me.

And on every one of these, may God have mercy on them all.

Verses on the Portrait of Chuffe

From the portrait in Ballymaloe drawing room

To please a good mistress I am drawn as you see –
and my crutch with my wounds thus expressed –
Shew a brace of hard balls in my body still be –
That will ever disquiet my rest.
Man's life and my length, are much of a size
Scarce either exceeds a good span
Menkind perpetually do me despise
And ye maids won't allow I'm a man.
Tho my inches are nine, besides a fair yard,
And my years are twenty and four,
Then pity my case which ye see is so hard
For I ne'er shall grow half an inch more.
Plain Dick: Noonane they called my dad
And for him t'was well enough
But I'm a much more dapper lad
So they call me Master Chuffe.

Changes to the Buildings at Ballymaloe Made by the Allens

1948–51   Renovation of Ballymaloe House; the architect was Ken Bayes. Bathrooms were put in and the kitchen moved from the wing into the alcove beside the dining room. A corridor was constructed behind the first-floor bedrooms which meant alterations to the shape of the staircase and stairwell. The house was rewired and dry-lined while central heating was put in.

1951-2   A bungalow was built in part of the walled garden for Mrs Elsie Hill, Myrtle Allen's mother. The architect was Pat Scott. It was subsequently lived in by the Bauer family, by Jim and Wendy Whelan, and by Rory and Hazel Allen.

1950–5   Philip and Lucy Pearce lived in the wing of Ballymaloe with their sons Stephen and Simon and daughter Sarah. Philip Pearce was a partner in Ivan's farming business but he began to make pottery in the greenhouse at Ballymaloe and then moved to the Glebe House at Kilmahon where he set up Shanagarry Pottery.

1955   The wing was let in the summer to English families for holidays.

1957   The swimming pool was built.

1964   The Yeats Room Restaurant opened. Trees were cut to make tables, an electric ring was purchased and an advertisement put in the *Cork Examiner*.

1965–6   An opening was made through the bawn wall to get from the drawing room to the cloakrooms behind. The bar was a large cupboard at the side of this opening.

1967   In order to become a guest house the courtyard buildings were converted to make bedrooms. Previously the building was a coach house and stables, with a loft above. There was a workshop used by Mr Bauer. The bedrooms in the house were gradually done up. There were two large rooms above the drawing and dining rooms which were the same size as the rooms below. The one over the drawing room was divided into two bedrooms. Over the dining room was the nursery which had been petitioned off so that three of the Allen children could sleep there. This also became two bedrooms – the Gold Room and Family Suite 1.

Ballymaloe became a guest house this year. With bedrooms the Allens could get a dispensing licence for drinks. They used the dispensing licence until 1996 but were then obliged to buy two contemporary licences.

1970   Discovery of the Patchwork Room. A member of the Arup Architectural Company was staying, who looked at the house from the outside and asked about a room which he knew must exist but into which there was no access. By breaking into the room from the corridor into the White Room, the Allens discovered this forgotten space. By building a staircase and opening the blocked window, another bedroom came into use – the Patchwork Room.

1980s   Five bedrooms were built on the lower ground level at the back of the house. A staircase was constructed with a glass wall and roof to go down to them.

Another bedroom was added to this row of rooms – the New West Room. The television room and toilets were constructed above this room which allowed the current bar to be created.

The conservatory and dining room were built over the new bedrooms.

1992   The tower was added to the bungalow in the garden by Rory and Hazel Allen.

1996   Four more bedrooms were added on the lower ground floor and the Long Room was constructed over them.

1998   An extension to the wine cellar was built. The boiler had been near the gate house but it was moved down into the farmyard and in the space which it had occupied new staff bedrooms were created.

2000   The Big Farm Shed replaced the old piggeries.

2004–5   A new boiler was installed with a self-feed mechanism.

2005   The lower yard of farm buildings was converted to make apartments.

2007   The silage store was converted to make a house known as the Tower.

2008   For many years, Joe Cronin had lived in the Steward's House which was now renovated and let. It is now lived in by Darren and Robyn Allen.

2007–9   The old granary was converted to create the Grainstore, a theatre and concert hall. This was a gradual process. The roof was replaced in 2007. After a pause the auditorium was finished for Róisín Allen's wedding in September 2009. The first concert was held a few months later. A meeting room and kitchen were subsequently added at the far end of the building.

The Walled Garden

The principal source for this appendix is the pamphlet by Susan Turner and the Ballymaloe Gardeners.

The Ballymaloe Ethos

The Ballymaloe ethos is to use the best seasonal and local ingredients in the kitchen. As far as possible the vegetables, herbs and fruit are grown in the walled garden. Recently the garden has been extended: to the west of the walled garden a new orchard has been planted which includes cider apples, cobnuts, plums, damsons and quince trees, with a walnut tree at the end of the path to give a focus.

Ballymaloe has a repertoire of traditional recipes to which new foods and ideas are often added. Based on the meat and fish available from local farmers and fishermen, and the vegetables which are just at their best in the garden, new menus are written every afternoon when the chefs see what has come in from their suppliers and they decide how to cook and combine the day's bounty.

The Walled Garden

The walls are ten feet high which protects the garden and gives it a microclimate of its own. South-facing walls reflect heat out onto the soil to a distance of seven inches and the stone also warms, so planting the fruit trees as espaliers against the south- and west-facing walls offers the best conditions for ripening fruit.

The glasshouse, built at the south of the garden, is used to propagate seeds and the young plants are potted on there and kept in the glasshouse until all fear of frost is over, which may be in mid-May. Once the young vegetables are planted out, the glasshouse is used for summer cuttings of shrubs and perennials as well as plants for the conservatory. Tomatoes, cucumbers, basil and chillies are all planted in the glasshouse where they can ripen. Vines under glass produce a crop of grapes. The warm air in the glasshouse is also good for drying onions and shallots as well as for saving seeds. Once the summer crop has been harvested, the glasshouse can be filled again with salad crops which will grow there safely through the winter.

Beside the glasshouse is the tool shed in which seeds are also stored, along with bulbs and tubers for planting, such as Jerusalem artichokes and potatoes.

Within the garden, the vegetables are carefully positioned. Perennials are planted at the edge where they can be kept weed-free but left undisturbed by the comings and goings of the annuals. The centre of the garden is regularly dug-over for the annuals crops which are part of a careful rotation.

The perennials include both vegetables and fruit. Asparagus likes the light soil at Ballymaloe and a bed of it has been kept going for half a century since the Allens first came to the house. This is a spring delicacy, harvested in April and May.

Seakale has to be forced early in the year by covering it with pots. Searching for light, it grows tall and pale with delicious stalks which are eaten from late March to the end of April.

As tubers, Jerusalem artichokes can be lifted and replanted, or left in the ground throughout the winter. They are tough and resistant to disease, so they remain in the same position from year to year.

The mouthwatering dessert trolley at Ballymaloe makes generous use of soft fruits. From July to October the garden sends in currants, gooseberries, tayberries and loganberries. There are autumn raspberries which will fruit until the first frosts and give the guests great pleasure. Rhubarb thrives in cool, moist conditions so has been planted alongside the shed.

The annual vegetable crops are in three groups. One third is brassicas – the cabbage family; one third is allium – the onion family; and one third of the space for annuals is taken up by other root vegetables such as carrots, with courgettes, pumpkins, beans and spinach.

With three blocks and therefore a three-year rotation, the plants get their best chance of health and vigour.

Ballymaloe House is always decorated with foliage and fresh flowers which are grown in the walled garden. The herbs grow beside them as the flowers attract bees and other insects. The larvae of hoverfly, lacewing and ladybirds devour greenfly and are a great help with pest control.

The flower garden is a delight in summer and among the flowers are edible blooms which are used in salad or for garnish.

Soil

At Ballymaloe, there is a focus on natural food, and healthy food grows from healthy soil. The garden is fertilised by compost and organic manure which feeds the microbes in the soil, enriching the nutrients and soil quality, which in turn feeds the plants. Bulky organic manures also improve the soil structure, helping to moderate its water retention.

The compost is a natural by-product of the kitchen waste. The gardeners get dung mixed with straw from local livestock farmers and from horse stables. The manure has to be stored until it breaks down sufficiently to use and it has to be covered to protect it from heavy rain or adulteration with weed seeds. Once it is well-rotted it makes a wonderful food source for the soil, leaving it rich in nutrients and well-aerated.

Green manures do the same job in a different way. These fast-growing plants are allowed to cover the ground before being dug back in to build up the soil structure. While they are growing they also provide a useful ground cover to protect the soil during winter rain and to smother weeds.

One of Ballymaloe's most valuable resources is the nearby coast. Seaweed was traditionally used as fertiliser in this area. It is high in trace elements and can be spread immediately after it is brought in from the beach, without waiting for it to rot, which other manures need. The trace elements give the plants yet another source of food, which in turn enriches the dishes which reach the tables in Ballymaloe's dining rooms.

Ballymaloe Owners and Occupiers

Baile Uí Mhaolmhuaidh was part of the estate of Cloyne cathedral

1304   Claimed by Simon le Blund, as his rightful inheritance from his father, Philip le Blund

1364   Held by Richard Whyte when the Cloyne Pipe Roll was compiled

1575   John FitzEdmund FitzGerald took a fee farm grant of the Cloyne cathedral lands

1580s   John FitzEdmund FitzGerald in residence at Ballymaloe

1612   Ballymaloe inherited by Sir John Óg, grandson of John FitzEdmund

1639   Cloyne see lands returned to the Bishop, the FitzGeralds received a lease instead of their grant

1640   Death of young Sir John, Ballymaloe inherited by his son Edmund

1641   During the rebellion, Edmund FitzGerald repossessed the Cloyne see lands

1645   Intense warfare in Imokilly. The FitzGeralds joined the Confederate Catholics and may have left the area

1657   Ballymaloe awarded to Roger Boyle, Viscount Broghill – later Earl of Orrery – by the parliament in Westminster

1660s   The Earl and Countess of Orrery reside at Ballymaloe occasionally

1669   Lady Powerscourt gave up a short lease of Ballymaloe which she held from her father

1679   Death of Orrery. Ballymaloe inherited by his second son, Colonel Henry Boyle

1700s   Richard Waller had a lease of Ballymaloe

1709   Edward Corker took a lease for perpetual renewal of Ballymaloe

1734   Death of Edward Corker, lease sold to Hugh Lumley

1755   Death of Hugh Lumley, lease inherited by his eldest son Henry Lumley who sold it to his brother William

1772   The head lease of Ballymaloe sold to Richard Longfield. William Lumley retained an underlease and lived at Ballymaloe

1782   Abraham Forster took a lease of Ballymaloe from Richard Longfield

1802   Death of Abraham Forster, the lease inherited by his son Clement John Forster

1842   Clement John's son, Abraham Thomas Forster sold the lease to John Litchfield

1906   The Litchfields bought the freehold of Ballymaloe

1944   Death of Myra Litchfield. Ballymaloe inherited by her nephew James Simpson

1947   James Simpson sold Ballymaloe to Ivan Allen of Imokilly Orchards

Select Bibliography

Abbreviations

CSPI   Calendar of State Papers Ireland, (London, 1860–1912).
Bod. Lib.   Bodleian Library, Oxford.
NLI   National Library of Ireland.
JCHAS   Journal of the Cork Historical and Archaeological Society.

Manuscript Sources

Bodleian Library
   Carte Ms. 45, f. 97, f. 162; Ms. 62, f. 152, f. 167; Ms. 221, ff. 235, 238 (Cloyne See lands)
Boole Library, University College Cork
   Inquisition Post Mortem: Sir John FitzEdmund FitzGerald – see *Ordnance Survey Inquisitions, Co. Cork*, 14/C 10, Co. Cork, vol. 1, p. 1 (on Royal Irish Academy microfilm)
Cork County Library
   Book of Survey and Distribution, Cork
National Archives Ireland
   Ms. 2449, Will of Richard Boyle, 1st Earl of Cork
   Ms. 2449, f. 12, 1st Earl of Orrery's right to erect a borough
National Library of Ireland
   Funeral Entries, Ulster King of Arms (Genealogical Office manuscript collection), microfilm, vol. 9, p. 232
   Lismore Papers, Ms. 13,236/14, Ms. 23,237/8, Ms. 43,266/6
   Orrery Papers, Ms. 32–36A
Shannon Papers, Ms. 13,295, Ms. 13,296, Ms. 13,298, Ms. 13,299

Printed Sources

A Census of Ireland, circa 1659, ed. S. Pender (Dublin, 2002)

Bolster, E., *A History of the Diocese of Cork*, vol. II (Shannon, 1991)

Borlase, E., *The History of the Execrable Irish Rebellion* (London, 1680)

Bottigheimer, K.S., *English Money and Irish Land: The Adventurers in the Cromwellian Settlement of Ireland* (New York, 1971)

Boyle, R., Earl of Cork, *The Lismore Papers* (London, 1886–8)

Brady, M., *Clerical and Parochial Records of Cork, Cloyne and Ross*, vols. I–II (Dublin, 1863–1864)

Burke, B., *Burke's Irish Family Records* (Buckingham, 2007)

Byrne, F., *Irish Kings and High-Kings* (London, 1973), esp. Ch. 5

Calendar of Entries in the Papal Registers Relating to Great Britain and Ireland: Papal Letters (London, 1893)

Caulfield, R., 'Proceedings', *The Journal of the Royal Historical and Archaeological Association of Ireland*, 4th ser., vol. 5, no. 42 (Apr. 1880), pp. 268–73

Caulfield, R., *The Annals of the Cathedral of St Coleman, Cloyne* (Cork, 1882)

Caulfield, R., ed., *The council book of the Corporation of the city of Cork, from 1609 to 1643, and from 1690 to 1800* (Guildford, 1876)

Childs, J., *The Williamite Wars* (London, 2007)

Collins, J.T., 'Ui Mac Caille, AD 177 to 1700', *JCHAS*, vol. L, 1945, pp. 31–9

Corish, P., 'The Cromwellian Regime, 1650–60', in T.W. Moody, F.X. Martin and F.J. Byrne (eds.), *A New History of Ireland, vol. III: Early Modern Ireland, 1534–1691* (Oxford, 1976)

Cox, Sir R., *The Autobiography of Rt. Hon. Sir Richard Cox, Lord Chancellor of Ireland* (London, 1860)

Cromwell, O., *Letters and Speeches*, T. Carlyle & S.C. Lomas, eds., vol. 1 (London, 1904)

Delany, V.T.H., 'English and Irish Land Law: Some Contrasts', *The American Journal of Comparative Law*, vol. 5, no. 3 (Summer, 1956), pp. 471–7

Dunlop, R., *Ireland under the Commonwealth*, vol. I (Manchester, 1913)

Edwards, N., 'The Archaeology of Early Medieval Ireland, c.400–1169', in D. Ó Cróinín, *A New History of Ireland*, vol. I (Oxford, 2005)

Facsimiles of national manuscripts of Ireland, eds. Rt. Hon. E. Sullivan and J.T. Gilbert (Dublin, 1874–84)

FitzGerald, B., *The Geraldines: An Experiment in Irish Government, 1169–1601* (London, 1951)

Fitzgerald, R.G., 'The Fitzgeralds of Rostellane in the County of Cork', *JRSAI*, vol. xxv, 1895, pp. 163–70

Godkin, J., *Ireland and Her Churches* (London, 1867), pp. 338–44

Gwynn, A. and Hadcock, R.N., *Medieval Religious Houses: Ireland* (Harlow, 1970)

Hayman, S. and Graves, J., *Unpublished Geraldine Documents* (Dublin, 1870–1) – also as a series in *Journal of the Royal Historical and Archaeological Association of*

Ireland, 3rd ser., vol. 1, pp. 356–416, 4th ser., vol. 1, pp. 591–616, vol. 4, pp. 14–52, 157–66

Henchion, R., *The Graveyard Inscriptions of the Cathedral Cemetery of Cloyne, Co. Cork* (Midleton, 2001)

Historical Manuscripts Commission, *Ormonde Mss.*, vol. 2 (London, 1902–20)

Hogan, E., *The Description of Ireland* (Dublin, 1878), http://www.dominicanscork.ie/friars/st-marys-church

Hull, V., 'Conall Corc and the Corco Luigde', *PMLA* (Journal of the Modern Language Association of America), 1947, pp. 887–909

Kearney, H.F., *Strafford in Ireland, 1633–41* (Manchester, 1959)

Larsen, A.C., 'The Exhibition: The Vikings in Ireland', in Larsen (ed.), *The Vikings in Ireland* (Roskilde, 2001)

Little, P., 'O'Brien, Murrough, first earl of Inchiquin', *Dictionary of National Biography* (Oxford, 2004)

Little, P., 'The Geraldine Ambitions of the First Earl of Cork', *Irish Historical Studies*, vol. 33, no. 130 (Nov. 2002), pp. 151–68

MacCotter, P. *Medieval Ireland* (Dublin, 2008)

MacCotter, P., 'Fitzgeralds', in P. Ó Loingsigh (ed.), *The Book of Cloyne* (Cloyne, 1993), pp. 79–100

MacCotter, P., *A History of the Medieval Diocese of Cloyne* (Blackrock, 2013)

MacLysaght, E., 'Commonwealth State Accounts', *Analecta Hibernica*, no. 15, Nov. 1944, pp. 236–7

McCafferty, J., *The Reconstruction of the Church of Ireland: Bishop Bramhall and the Laudian Reforms, 1633–1641* (Cambridge, 2007)

McCormack, A., *The Earldom of Desmond, 1463–1583: The Decline and Crisis of a Feudal Lordship* (Dublin, 2005)

MacSwiney Brugha, M., *History's Daughter: A Memoir from the Only Child of Terence MacSwiney* (Dublin, 2005)

MacSwiney, M., *Letters to Angela Clifford* (Belfast, 1996)

Mitchell, B., *A New Genealogical Atlas of Ireland* (Baltimore, 1986)

Monk, M.A. and Sheehan, J., *Early Medieval Munster* (Cork, 1998)

Murphy, D., *Cromwell in Ireland* (Dublin, 1883)

Murphy, E., 'Phaire, Robert', *Dictionary of Irish Biography* (Cambridge, 2009)

Murphy, J.A., 'The Expulsion of the Catholics from Cork in 1644', *JCHAS*, no. 69, 1964, pp. 123–31

Murphy, J.A., 'The Politics of the Munster Protestants, 1641–1649', *JCHAS*, no. 76, 1971, pp. 1–20

Murphy, J.A., 'The Sack of Cashel', *JCHAS*, no. 70, 1965, pp. 55–62

Murphy, M., 'The Royal Visitation of Cork, Cloyne and Ross, and the College of Youghal', *Archivium Hibernicum*, vol. 2 (1913), pp. 173–215

Myrtle Allen: A Life in Food, RTÉ television documentary 2015, (InProduction TV)

Nicholls, K., 'The Development of Lordship in Co. Cork, 1300–1600', in P. O'Flanagan and C.G. Buttimer, *Cork: History and Society* (Dublin, 1993)

Ó Buachalla, L., 'The Uí Liatháin and Their Septlands', *JCHAS*, 1939, pp. 28–36

O'Brien, A.F., *The Impact of the Anglo-Normans on Munster* (Carrigtwohill, 1997)

O'Carroll, G., *The Earls of Desmond*: *The Rise and Fall of a Munster Lordship* (Tralee, 2013)

O'Hart, J., *The Irish and Anglo-Irish Landed Gentry when Cromwell Came to Ireland* (Dublin, 1884)

Parliamentary Papers, 1780–1849, vol. 9, p. 133, for May 1842

Pearce, S., *Warrior Spirit* (Cork, 2013)

Pender, S., 'The Uí Liatháin Genealogies from the Book of Ballymote', *JCHAS*, 1938, pp. 32–8

Ranger, T., 'Richard Boyle and the Making of an Irish Fortune, 1588–1614', *Irish Historical Studies*, vol. 10, no. 39 (Mar. 1957), pp. 257–97

Richter, M., *Medieval Ireland*: *The Enduring Tradition* (Dublin, 1988)

Sawyer, P. (ed.), *Oxford Illustrated History of the Vikings* (Oxford, 1997)

Smith, C., *The Antient and Present State of the County and City of Cork*, vols. I & II (Dublin, 1774)

Simington, R.C., *The Transplantation to Connacht, 1654–58* (Shannon, 1970)

Southern Reporter and Cork Commercial Courier, 4 Sept. 1841

Sweetman, H.S. and Handcock, G.F., *Calendar of Documents Relating to Ireland*, 5 vols. (London, 1875–86)

Taylor, G. and Skinner, A., *Maps of the Roads of Ireland* (Dublin, 1977)

Thurloe, J., *State Papers*, vol. VII (London, 1742)

Townshend, D., *The Life and Letters of the Great Earl of Cork* (London, 1904)

Tuckey, F.H., *The County and City of Cork Remembrancer* (Cork, 1837)

Watt, J., *The Church in Medieval Ireland* (Dublin, 1998)

Welch, P. (ed.), *Concise Oxford Companion to Irish Literature* (Oxford, 2000)

Index

Abbot, William 103
Act of Settlement of 1662 72
Allen
  family tree 139
  Ivan 123-4, 126-9, 131-4
  Myrtle (née Hill) 126-7, 129, 131-4,
    136-7
  Wendy 130, 133-4, 136 also see
    Whelan
  Natasha 130
  Tim 130, 135-6
  Rory 130, 136-7
  Yasmin 130, 133
  Fern 130, 133, 135-6
  Darina (née O'Connell) 135-7
  Hazel (née Lalor) 135-6, 138
  Rachel (née O'Neill) 138
Askeaton 45

Ballinacurra 21, 42, 47, 123
Ballycotton 62-4, 126; fishermen 25,
  64, 81; castle 43
Ballyduff, Cloyne 125, 132
Ballymaloe
  name 1, 21
  land ownership 17, 23-4, 27, 33-4,
    36, 38, 41, 56, 59, 63-5, 82, 73,
    103, 114
  tower house and turret 24, 30-3
  bawn wall 31-2, 41, 58

well 1, 33, 58
Sir John FitzEdmund's house 48, 57,
  87-8, 96
garden and plants 96-7, 106-7, 119,
  124-5, 136, 146-8
hospitality at 57-9, 62-3, 81
Queen Anne wing 87-8
furniture and furnishings 81, 87,
  90-1, 112, 188
stables and stable yard 58, 87-9, 102
farming at 13, 23, 108, 110-1, 119,
  121-2, 125-6, 128-9, 131, 134
farmyard 33, 41, 71, 137
Morrison extension 96
front façade, rebuilding of, early 19th
  century 102
sale of, in 1870 110, in 1883 111, in
  1947 127
kitchen 32, 48, 107, 119, 125-6
restaurant at, (Yeats Room) 132-4
Guest House 134-6
renovations 1947-9 129
extensions by Allen family 134, 137,
  144-5
Ballymaloe beg 87, 111
Ballymaloe Cookery School 135-7
Ballymaloe Cottage 125, 127
Ballymaloe Relish 136
Ballymaloe Shop 125, 136
Ballymartyr 28, 66

Ballyoughtera church 63

Barnabrow 33, 124

Barry, family of 19, 31 62; Philip de 19; Ellen, see FitzGerald, Ellen; Lord Barry 38, 42, 44

Barryscourt 31, 39, 43 47

Bauer family 132, 134

Bayes, Ken, architect 129

Bennett, John 123

Berkeley, George, bishop of Cloyne 79

Betaghs 23, 25

Blarney Castle 71, 73

Blund
Eliza le 22; Philip le 22; Simon le 22-3, 111

Boyle
family tree 76
Henry, Colonel 82-4, 90
Henry, 1st Earl of Shannon 84, 90, 92
Mary, Lady (née O'Brien) 82-3, 90
Margaret, (née Howard), 1st countess of Orrery 80, 83
Richard, 1st earl of Cork 47, 56, 60-1, 63, 67, 73, 75, 77-80
Roger, viscount Broghill, 1st earl of Orrery 68, 73, 75, 77-80; military career 68, 7-2, 78; land 75; lord president of Munster 75, 77, 82; children 80

Brocquy, Louis le 7, 134

Bronze Age forts 7

Bronze Age remains 3; at Carrigacrump 6; at Knockane 4, lunula at Midleton 6

Burghley, William Cecil, Lord 44, 49

Butler
family 42, 44, 57; James, 12th Earl & 1st Duke of Ormond 78

Butter, made at Ballymaloe 125

Caragh Lake, Kerry 123, 128

Carew family 47, 49, 52, 61, 82

Carrigacotter 46, 75

Castle Mary, Cloyne 98, 104, 123

Castle Redmond 47

Castle Richard 28, 31, 36

Castlehaven, James Touchet, 3rd earl of 69-70

Castlelyons 8

Castlemartyr 21, 28, 33, 36, 39, 42, 44, 57, 60, 63, 66, 70, 73, 75, 82-4, 90, 107

Cecil, Robert, 1st Earl of Salisbury 49-51

Charleville 75, 77, 81-2

Chichester, Sir Arthur, Lord Deputy of Ireland 61-2

Chore, abbey 40, 42; castle 42, 47

Chuffe 89, 97, 105, 135, 143

Clancy, Liam 134

Clonmel 22

Clonmult, Ballyonane, Ballybranock & Geoghans – land holdings 131

Cloyne Castle 24-5, 28, 30, 43, 50, 56, 79

Cloyne, early Christian foundation 9, 12; church lands 12, 17, 21, 24, 29, 30, 40-1, 59, 61-4, 78-9, 91; fee farm grant 35, 40-1, 61; monastery 13-4, 17, 19; cathedral 22, 25, 30, 97, 110, 123; bishop 21-5, 27-8, 52, 63, 77-8, 91; chapter 21-2; dean 21-2, 28-30, 34, 36; manor 25, 64-5

Cloyne House 41, 79

Cloyne round tower 18

Coipré, king of Cashel 9

Colmán Mac Léinín, of Cloyne, saint 9, 12, 141

Condon, family of 47

Confederate Catholics of Ireland 65-6, 68, 70, 72

Conner family of west Cork 93, 95, 98

Cork city 21, 39, 43, 71, 84, 93, 95-6, 99, 100

Cork Corporation and business
    community 93, 95, 99-100, 103
Corkbeg 39, 47
Corker, Edward, MP, of Ballymaloe
    84-7, 89-90, 95, 100
Corker, Edward, MP, of Ratoath, Co.
    Louth 85, 87, 90-1
Corker family tree 86
Corker, Margaret (née Wallis) 85, 89-90
Costabadie, Hugh de 127
Costobadie, Joan de (née Simpson) 119,
    122, 126
Coxwell-Rogers 124
Crawford Art Gallery 136
Creed, Charles 124
Croker, Crofton 4
Cromwell, Oliver 66, 70-3
Cronin, Joe 131-2, 134

Desmond, kingdom of 19; earls of 27,
    36, 45, 63; James, 15th earl 38-9,
    42-5; James, 'Tower earl' 49-51
Dilkes, Sir Thomas 84
Dillon, Captain George 77
Donogh, Honor Ní 35
Doolin, Dan 121

Elizabeth I 35-6, 40, 43-5, 49, 51, 53

Farming, early medieval 13-4
FitzGerald, family 26-7, 29 n. 33, 37,
    79, 94; family tree 37; poem by
    Thomas Davis 79
    Edmund FitzJames, Dean of Cloyne
        34, 36
    David FitzJames 29
    Edmund, son of Sir John
        FitzEdmund 41, 51, 56-7, 60
    Edmund, son of Sir John Og 62-3
    Edmund of Castlemartyr, son of
        the last seneschal 46, 60, 63, 66,
        68-71

Ellen (née Barry), wife of Sir John Og
    62-3
Honor, (née O'Brien) wife of Sir John
    FitzEdmund 41, 48, 56
Honora, Lady, of Castlemartyr and
    Ballymaloe 44, 57, 60-3
James FitzDavid, Dean of Cloyne 34
James FitzMaurice, 'the arch traitor'
    39, 41-4, 57
James, of Ballyhonock, agent 64-5,
    78
James, son of Sir John FitzEdmund
    48
Sir John FitzEdmund, Dean of
    Cloyne 30, 35-60 passim; lands
    of 38, 41, 44-7, 49, 57, 61; support
    for the crown 39, 43, 51-2, 57;
    Sheriff of County Cork 39, 46;
    grants from the crown 39-40,
    43-4, 46; carved stones 41, 53, 58,
    87, 96, 122; farming and business
    enterprises 47; children 41, 48,
    59-60; indicted for high treason
    49; knighthood 52; surrender and
    re-grant 53, 56; will 59, 62, 64;
    tomb 59
Sir John Óg, son of Edmund of
    Ballymaloe 60, 62-4; will and
    codicil 64-5, 78
John FitzEdmund, Seneschal of
    Imokilly 36, 38-9, 42, 44, 46, 57
Maurice 19
Thomas, son of Sir John FitzEdmund
    62
FitzMaurice, Patrick, 19th Baron of
    Kerry 61, 63-4
Flynn, Thady, Dean of Cloyne 35, 38
Forge at Ballymaloe beg 125
Forster, family 99, family tree 101;
    Clement, father of Mary Lumley
    98-100; Abraham 99-102;
    Charlotte (née Rowland) 100, 102;

Forster (cont.):
    Catherine (née Rowland) 100, 102;
    Clement John 102-4; Margaret
    (née Cuthbert) 103; Abraham
    Thomas 103, 105; Francis 103;
    Thomas 104
Fota 18, 123
French Church Street, Cork 93

Garrettstown, Kinsale 103, 105
Gernon, Luke 57-9
Giant Irish deer, Megaloceros giganteus
    1-3, 97, 118
Grainstore at Ballymaloe 122, 137, 145
Griffin family 121

Harp, the FitzGerald of Cloyne 62, 135,
    142
Henry II 21-2
Henry VIII 34, 39
Hewson, family of 107, 112
Hill, architects, 126; Arthur 126,
    136; Henry Houghton 126, 132,
    Elizabeth (Elsie) 132
Hodnett 47
Huguenots 93, 95, 99

Ightermurragh 81-2
Imokilly 9, 19, 25, 27-8, 30, 34-5, 38,
    46, 68, 70, 79
Imokilly Orchards 128, 130-2
Inchiquin manor 22
IRA 116
Irwin, Colonel John 84

Jester, portrait of 89, 105, 135
Jordan, Bishop of Cloyne 28
Justiciar's visit 1301 21-2

Kerricurrihy 57
Kilkenny 66
Killarney, steamer 104

Kilmahon, parish 16, 19, 89, 107;
    Church and graveyard 16; Glebe
    House 130
Kinoith 112, 122-3, 127-8, 132, 135,
    137
Kinsale, battle of 51-2
Knocknannus, battle of 70
Kylgallan 27

Land Acts – sales under 113-4
Landed Estates Court 110
Lismore 18, 56, 68
Litchfield, family tree 109; drapery
    business 106; John 105-6, 108,
    110; William, father of John 106-7;
    Albina 106-7; Sarah (née Hewson)
    107-8, 110, 114; William, son of
    John 107-8, 110-1, 115-6, 125;
    Caroline 108, 110-1, 114-6, 122-3,
    125; Maurice 108, 110; Myra,
    (Helen Maria) 108, 111, 114, 116,
    122-3, 125-6; Jane, see Simpson;
    Jack (John) 108, 111, 114, 116, 125
Longfield family 95, 100, 103-5, 110-1,
    113; Richard, Lord Longueville 95,
    99, 101, 103
Lumley, family tree 94, family of 99-
    100; Hugh 92-3, 95-7; Henry 93;
    Henry, son of Hugh 97-8; Mary
    (née Forster) 98, 100, 102; Mary
    (née Musgrave) 95; William, son of
    Hugh 198, 102

Mac Tíre 19
MacCarthy family 19, 28, 71
MacCridan 62
Macra na Feirme 131
Madonna, or Virgin, statue of in
    Dominican church 61
Mahon or Macha 16
Mail coach 103
Mallow 71, 95

Manaig 17-8
McCotter family 47
McSwiney, Muriel (née Murphy) 115
Meredith family, of Barnabrow 124
Mhaolmhuaidh, or Mo Lua, of
	Ballymaloe 1, 13; saint 12-3
Midleton 47, 111-3
Mills 14
Milshane 33
Mogeely 25, 34, 38
Morgan, Helen (née Simpson) 117-9,
	125-7
Morgan, Tom 127
Morrison, John of Midleton, architect
	90
Mountjoy, Charles Blount, Baron 51-2
Moyle, Captain 57
Munster rebellions 38-9, 42-5

Neill, Larry, coachman 113, 119
Newtown School, Waterford 123, 128,
	132

O'Brien, family 19; Dermod, 5th baron
	Inchiquin 63; Murrough, 1st earl of
	Inchiquin 63, 67-9, 71-2, 77-8, 80,
	82, 84; Ellen (née FitzGerald), wife
	of Dermond 5th baron Inchiquin
	63, 67; Honor, wife of Sir John
	FitzEdmund, see FitzGerald
O'Connell, Rory 135-7
O'Neill, Hugh, Earl of Tyrone 49, 51
Oldfield, Eric 127
Oldfield, Priscilla (née Simpson) 118,
	122, 126-7
Owenacurra River 42

Parliament, Dublin 45
Payne, Moira (née Hill) 132; George,
	Colonel 132; Desmond 132
Pearce, Philip, 129-131; Lucy, (née
	Crocker) 129-131; Stephen 129

Peckham project 130
Penn Wm, 86-7; family 89, 111
Penrose-Fitzgerald 110, 115-6
Perrier, Sir Anthony 99
Perrott, John, President of Munster 39
Phaire, Colonel 71
Pipe Roll of Cloyne 24-6
Poer, John le 22
Power family 25, 46
Powerscourt, Elizabeth, Lady (née
	Boyle) 81-2

Quakers 72, 86, 128-9, 131-2

Raincock, John and family 93, 95
Raleigh, Sir Walter 42-3, 47-8, 50, 56,
	75
Rathcoursey 22, 102
Rebellion, of 1641 65-6; of 1798
	100-1
Red House, Shangarry 126
Ridney, John, blacksmith 121
Roberts, Harry 131
Roche family 28
Rooskagh River 30, 33
Rooskah Valley Mushrooms 131
Rostellan 69, 80, 110
Rowland family 104-5, 107, 112, 123,
	135
Rugge, Henry 67

Saunders, Colonel Peter 72-3, 75
Saxey, William 48-9
Scott, Pat 130, 132, 134
Seetree, John 95
Seneschal of Imokilly 278, 30, 33-4, 36,
	38, 42, 44, 46, 57
Shanagarry 16, 22, 25, 73, 75, 867, 89,
	108
Shanagarry Farm (Imokilly Orchards)
	124, 126-9, 131-2, 136
Shanagarry Pottery 130

Shannon estate (Castlemartyr) 96, 99, 101, 104, 113

Sheanlis 34

Shehan, Mathew, Bishop of Cork and Cloyne 40, 61

Sidney, Sir Henry 39-40

Simpson, Charles Sussex 110-1; Jane (née Litchfield) 108, 110, 122, 124-5; Dorothy 110, 122, 124-5; Jim (Captain James) 110, 116-9, 121, 123-8; Norah 122, 125, Marion (née Windeyer) 116-9, 121, 123-5, 127; Helen, see Morgan; Joan, see Costabadie; Priscilla, see Oldfield

Sinn Féin 115

Skiddy, Roger, Bishop of Cork and Cloyne 35-6, 61

Skiddy, Thomas, agent 65

Spain and Spanish troops 46, 49, 51-2

Spolasco, Baron 104

St Leger, lord presidents of Munster, Sir Warham 42-3, Sir William 67-8

Stone Age axe-heads 3-4

Strangman, Thomas and Sarah 112; Wilson 112-4, 122-4, 126-7, 132; Lydia 112, 122-3, 132; John Robert 112, 114

Swaffham, John de 24

Synge, George, bishop of Cloyne 63, 65, 79

Táin Bó Cúailnge 7

Tax 21-2, 82, 111, 123, 126

Tower-houses 30, 58

Uí Liatháin 8

Uí MacCaille 9

Veal, Morris and Ned 121

Vikings 18-9

Waller, Richard 84

Wallis, Colonel Peter 72-3, 75, 86-7

Wallop, Sir Henry 45

Walsh, Davey 116; Margaret and Nellie 122

Walsyngham, Sir Francis 43-4

Waterford 21, 62, 70, 75, 112, 123

Wentworth, Thomas, 1st earl of Strafford 63-4

Whelan, Jim 134, Wendy 133-4, 136

White, also, Whyte, Whyt 22, 27, 34, 38; Richard 25-6

Whitegate 18

Williamite war 83-5

Windele, John 5

Windeyer, Sir Charles and family 118

Womanagh River 28

Wood Richard 131

Yeats Room, see Ballymaloe, restaurant

Youghal 21, 42, 50, 52, 58, 67-8, 70, 91, 99, 103, 107, 127